About The Struggl

CW00669954

Winner 2003 M&C Prize for Prose

1993 was an ominous year for St. Lucia. It was the year the European Community would become a unified market, thereby throwing into doubt the continuance of the preferential treatment bananas were enjoying on the UK market. The nation's worse fears were confirmed when the year began with banana prices falling below most farmers' cost of production. Farmers responded. They demanded a guarantee minimum price of 30 cents per pound of bananas, the dissolution of the allegedly corrupt board of directors of the St. Lucia Banana Growers' Association (SLBGA), the appointment of a new board and the streamlining of SLBGA operations to return to farmers a larger share of banana export receipts.

No one heeded the farmers' demands. So on October 5, 1993, they went on strike, not only refusing to harvest their bananas, but taking drastic actions to ensure the fruits of non-striking farmers never reach port. The Strike, which wasn't without precedent, was quite understandable. However, what no one could have predicted was that it would not only end with the deaths of two farmers, but would signal a shift in the political and socioeconomic structure of the country.

One comes away from a reading of The Struggle For Survival with the feeling that the plight of farmers was nothing less than an allegory of the history of the island, and the deaths an omen of the future of the banana industry in St. Lucia.

The Struggle for Survival is history that reads like a novel. The book is a multilayered and dynamic narrative of the history, politics, culture and economics of St. Lucia. With just one glance through history, the book captures the essence of St. Lucian society.

It is a must read for all students of St. Lucian and Caribbean history, because in tracing how the banana industry has contributed to the socioeconomic and political development of the country, the book provides a compelling narrative on why and how St. Lucia became the way it is.

"The Struggle For Survival, although obviously well researched, is an easy-to-read intriguing story of the social and political development of St. Lucia. The book lays the basis for critical examinations of the legacy of European plantocracy and a determination of modern history's perception of the descendant of African slaves in the Caribbean as victor or victims in our political destiny. The Struggle For Survival held my attention from beginning to end."
—Travis Weekes, Author of Let There Be Jazz

"In Dr. Reynolds, St. Lucia has produced another writer of the calibre, or of even deeper essence than Nobel Laureate V. S. Naipaul."
— Peter Lansiquot, CARICOM economist and diplomat

THE STRUGGLE
FOR
SURVIVAL

Also by Anderson Reynolds

My Father Is No Longer There (memoir, 2019)

The Stall Keeper (novel, 2017)

Death by Fire (novel, 2001)

Other Jako Books

A Lesson On Wings (poetry, 2019) Modeste Downes

The Brown Curtains (novel, 2006) Clive Sankardayal

Phases (poetry, 2005) Modeste Downes

Rhythms of the Ghetto (poetry, 2004) Ken Ballantyne

THE STRUGGLE
FOR
SURVIVAL

an historical, political, and socioeconomic perspective of St. Lucia

Anderson Reynolds

JAKO BOOKS

New York, London, Toronto, Vieux Fort

Published in the United States by Jako Books, a division of Jako Productions.

Third Jako Books Edition, June 2018

Cataloging-in-Publication Data
Reynolds, Anderson.
    The Struggle For Survival : an historical, political, and socioeconomic perspective of St. Lucia / Anderson Reynolds.
    p. cm.
    Includes bibliographical references and index.
    LCCN: 2002113166
    ISBN-13: 978-0-9704432-8-1

    1. Saint Lucia—History.   I. Title.

F2100.R49 2003   972.9843
                        QBI02-201031

Printed in the United States of America

This book is dedicated to my father, St. Brice Reynolds, who, while on his early morning walk on June 6, 2002, was killed by an out of control vehicle. He was seventy-eight and in good health.

Contents

Foreword

When the great fire of 1948 devastated the capital, Castries, a North American magazine carried an article on the tragic event which began with the observation that "Disaster is no stranger to Saint Lucia."

Indeed, not, and Dr. Anderson Reynolds, in this, his second published work, has chronicled in dramatic se-quence, those disasters and misfortunes which, periodi-cally, have affected the island from its discovery down to the present day.

Dr. Reynolds has a great fascination for history and, like the German philosophers, Hegel and Oswald Spengler, believes that history has an uncanny way of repeating itself, and woe to those who take no notice of historical events. Dr. Reynolds demonstrates how, in Saint Lucia, because of that failure to take note and to learn from the lessons of history, Saint Lucians have brought about misfortunes upon themselves which could have been avoided. From slavery to colonialism, but, more specifically, in contemporary events—sugar strikes, banana farmers' strikes and other industrial ac-tions by workers. With that Lemming-like mentality Saint Lucians have paid the price for ignoring the lessons of the past.

What is it about the concern with history that has been occupying Saint Lucian contemporary writers? Dr. Anderson Reynolds In his first novel, Death by Fire, Dr. Earl Long in his sec-ond novel, Voices From A Drum, Mr. Michael Aubertin with his novel, Neg Marron, and Mr. McDonald Dixon in his first novel Season Of Mist, all have been dealing with certain aspects of the Saint Lucian historical experience. That "backward glance" it has occurred to me, is not simply an effort to come to terms with that historical experience, but, more importantly, to establish who and what we are, what makes us tick. It is, in a very definite way, to establish the Saint Lucian personality, the Saint Lucian national and cultural identity.

Saint Lucians, like Dr. Reynolds are beginning to look at their island and at the development of them-selves as a people.

This is an invaluable book, a source of much infor-mation. Much scholarly research has gone into the writ-ing of this work. More, it seeks to clarify issues and contemporary events, issues and events which have become somewhat blurred in the minds of the people, and in certain cases, misrepresented for political pur-poses, and totally unknown to the younger generation who take so many things for granted, and therefore un-aware of the struggles, often violent and sanguine, which have brought Saint Lucia from slavery, then a poor, backward colonial territory to the relative prosperity which the island enjoys today. Yet, despite that relative prosperity, Dr. Reynolds is apprehensive of the future, always bearing in mind the lessons of history.

Jacques Compton

Fellow of the Royal Society of Arts

Chavalier De L'Ordre Des Arts Et Des Lettre

Acknowledgments

I would like to thank Mr. Jacques Compton, Mr. Ken-neth Springer, Mr. Derrick Redman and Mrs. Bushell for their thoughtful and meticulous edit and proof read of this manuscript. The Struggle For Survival has benefitted much from their suggestions.

THE STRUGGLE FOR SURVIVAL

"Native Huts" St. Lucia, B.W.I.

1

The Strike

The deaths in the valley were the culmination of a banana strike that started three days before. Yet in the days preceding the strike there were many calls admonishing farmers against it. The Prime Minister, Mr. John Compton, himself a banana farmer, the St. Lucia Banana Growers' Association (SLBGA), the National Farmers' Association (NFA), the Chamber of Commerce, the Acting High Commissioner, the Civil Service Association, and many private citizens, all called for reason, level headedness, and patience. Farmers, they advised, should resolve their grievances through meetings and discussions because, after all, a strike against the SLBGA, which ultimately was owned by farmers, was in effect farmers striking against themselves. They warned that if farmers strike, the SLBGA would have to compensate Geest, the banana shipping company, for its ship arriving at port to collect fruit but leaving empty, and nonstriking farmers for harvested fruit they could not take to market. All these monies would eventually come out of farmers' proceeds from future sales of bananas. But more importantly, a strike could jeopardize the trade arrangement that afforded St. Lucian bananas preferential treatment on the UK market.

In spite of all these admonishments and warnings, Tuesday, October 5, 1993, activist farmers did not only go on strike, refusing to harvest their bananas, but they also took steps to ensure that the fruit of nonstriking farmers never reached the ports.

Besides burning the banana sheds of farmers who refused to strike, striking farmers set up barricades of felled trees, burning tires, large rims, 10 to 14 wheel truck chassis, and derelict vehicles across feeder roads and at various points on the East Coast Highway, rendering them impassible. At the southern village of Desruisseaux, tucked in the interior of the island, farmers stoned tractor-operating police officers attempting to dismantle barricades. In the turmoil, one officer was injured and was rushed to hospital. All over the east coast, no sooner had police officers removed a block-ade, protesters would erect replacement barriers, even if it meant working overnight. The situation got so seri-ous that the Police Department discouraged motorist from using the East Coast Highway, the SLBGA cautioned nonstriking farmers against taking fruit to market, and hotels at the northern end of the island encouraged vacationers arriving at the southern town of Vieux Fort to take air shuttles to the northern city of Castries, instead of the customary ground taxies. By Wednesday, the second day of the strike, it appeared that bands of farmers turned engineers, armed with stones, bottles, cutlasses, and pent up anger had taken over the island.

So by Thursday, October 7, the third day of the strike, the stage was set for the afternoon showdown that brought death to the valley. The crowds at the barri-cades were getting larger as farmers and their support-ers were now joined by the unemployed, those seeking excitement, entertainment and bounty, even. Fueled by success and added numbers, farmers were getting bold-er and more confident. The police were overworked, frustrated, and lacking sleep. The essence of carrying out law and order was control. Yet it appeared that farmers, not the police, were the ones in control.

School children were not getting to schools, workers were not getting to their jobs, the sick were not getting to hospitals, tourists were not getting to miracle beaches and fantasy hotels, the nation's cargo was waiting impatiently at ports for distribution.

The citizenry, those not too sympathetic to the cause of banana farmers and those who thought that farmers had taken their grievances too far, were demanding that something be done. Fear for life, fear of loss of business, fear of loss of tourists dollars was mounting.

So the Prime Minister, himself a banana farmer, spoke up. He said that the dispute between farmers and the SLBGA had been taken over by "certain elements who had been particularly active in the Mabouya Valley." Accordingly, police reinforcements were dispatched with instructions to take all necessary measures to restore law and order. With the police so armed the stage was set for the final showdown in the valley.

2

The East Coast Highway

I f farmers' intentions were to bring the country to its knees, they couldn't have targeted a better highway than the stretch of the East Coast Highway joining Castries in the North to Vieux Fort in the South. The eastern half of the island accounted for the lion's share of the country's economic activity, was home to more than 78 percent of its population, and supplied the greater part of its banana output. Therefore, any disruption of the flow of traffic between Vieux Fort and Castries, along the East Coast Highway, was bound to have a significant negative impact on the economy.

Castries was the capital of the country and together with its environs was by far the nation's most important town. It was the island's busiest commercial center and as home (Castries and adjoining Rodney Bay and Gros Islet) to most of its hotels and best restaurants, it represented the nucleus of the tourism industry. St. Lucia had two seaports and two airports. Vigie Airport, the airport found in Castries, renamed George F.L. Charles, in honor of one of the founding father's of the nation, was the busiest of the two, and Port Castries was one of the busiest ports in the Eastern Caribbean. Not surprisingly, more than 40 percent of the island's 156,000 inhabitants resided in the district of Castries.

Vieux Fort was second only to Castries in importance. The town was the commercial center of the south of the island, and as the industrial capital of St. Lucia was home to one of the highest concentrations of industrial activity in the Eastern Caribbean. The island's international airport was also located there and its seaport was operated as a Caribbean container transshipment center.

Along the West Coast Highway, gigantic mountains rose to great heights and descended to great depths into the Caribbean Sea. So majestic was the landscape that to the onlooker it seemed impossible that such a spectacle had come about by chance and not by design. However, the same terrain that made the eyes gaze in wonderment left little room for settlement and agriculture, and made road construction hazardous and almost impossible. Hence, along the west coast, population and economic activity had remain sparse.

However, in the days before motor vehicles and before the Island had a developed road system, when travel by sea was the norm, the west coast held greater prominence. Being on the leeward side of the island, its waters were easier to navigate than those of the east coast, and thus it lent itself to settlement. The west coast town of Soufrière, home to the Pitons, the island's majestic twin peaks, one of the wonders of the Caribbean and a world heritage preserve candidate, was once not only the capital of St. Lucia but also its most important settlement. Up till 2002 Soufrière was the only town or village on the island that gave the impression that some degree of planning had gone into its construction.

In Soufrière, sea, sky, mountains, quaintness and rusticity came together in such a way as to give the impression that the town and its setting were designed to optimize its appeal to the eye. Although all parts of St. Lucia were possessed with the picturesqueness that would make the whole island worthy of a national park, it was at Soufrière that the island entered its finest glory, and it was the Pitons of Soufrière that the Caribs had chosen as their gods.

Approaching Soufrière, one got the distinct feeling that one was entering a different town in a different country; it felt and looked like no other settlement on the island. Not surprisingly, tourism was the town's most important industry. Still, besieged by the Pitons and other gigantic land masses, Soufrière had little room for expansion, so as if suspended in space, time, and distance, it had remained about the same size for decades, such that not only Castries, but also the towns of Vieux Fort and Gros Islet had surpassed it in importance and population.

North of Soufrière, along the West Coast Highway, were the villages of Canaries and Anse La Raye. Villages that had come into existence partly because they were stopovers for travelers plying between Castries and Soufrière, back in the days when movement between coastal villages was done mostly by sea. By 2002 these villages were among the poorest on the island and probably owed their continued existence more to their proximity to Castries than to any inherent economic viability.

St. Lucia was divided into ten districts, five along the East Coast Highway (Gros Islet, Castries, Dennery, Micoud, and Vieux Fort) and the other five along the West Coast Highway (Laborie, Choiseul, Soufrière, Ca¬naries, and Anse La Raye). The five least populated districts were those along the West Coast Highway, and Canaries with a population of only 1,935 was the least populated of them all.

Now, if one were to block the East Coast Highway, motorists traveling to either Vieux Fort or Castries could turn around and travel along the west coast. However, this hadn't been a very palatable alternative because the distance from Castries to Vieux Fort along the west coast was ten miles longer along a roadway that was much more treacherous and in a worse state of disrepair. By 1995 most of the west coast road was enlarged and improved. Still, right up to 2002, the section of the West Coast Highway linking Vieux Fort to Soufrière was one of the narrowest and most neglected stretches of highway on the island.

3

It's Bananas Stupid

I f in 1993 someone had wanted to cripple the country's economy by undermining a single sector, they would have been hard pressed to find any other crop or for that matter any other economic activity that would have served better than the banana industry. Banana was by far the most important crop. It occupied 40 percent of all crop lands, and its 1990 production of 135 thousand tonnes (all time peak) contrasted sharply with the five thousand tonnes of copra obtained from coconuts, the second most important crop.

The banana industry was a major source of income. In 1990, it accounted for 10.3 percent of the Gross Domestic Product (GDP), exceeding the contributions of both tourism (9.6 percent) and manufacturing (8.2 percent). In fact, only wholesale and retail trade, transport and communications, and producers of government services contributed more to GDP than the banana industry. GDP aside, the banana industry was estimated to inject roughly three million dollars each week into the economy, and for every 10 percent increase in banana export earnings, government revenues were said to increase by an estimated 6.5 percent.

Banana featured even more prominently in the nation's trade balances and thus its foreign exchange earnings. Its exports in 1990 earned $187 million, representing 91 percent of agricultural exports and 58 percent of domestic exports. Moreover, banana exports were estimated to contribute more than $171 million in foreign exchange earnings.

As a source of employment banana was second to none. In 1990, about twenty thousand people (including registered banana growers, field workers and employees of the St. Lucia Banana Growers' Association) were directly employed in the banana industry, and another 40,000 persons were thought to be indirectly dependent on the industry for employment and income. In contrast, the combined (direct) employment of tourism (Hotels and Restaurants) and manufacturing was less than 13,000 workers.

However impressive these statistics, they did not tell the whole story. Compared with hotels and manufacturing firms, many of which were foreign owned, most of the earnings from bananas remained in the country. Moreover, evidence suggested that banana earnings were circulated more extensively and more deeply than the earnings of most other sectors. That was why economists agreed that the banana industry had a significant income multiplier effect. The contributions of the banana industry were not only substantial, but its income effects were pervasive. The banana industry touched all segments of the society.

There was another economic principle at work that made the contributions of bananas even more important to the economic health of the nation. For a while now economists had known that the lower one's income the greater the propensity to consume from an additional dollar of income. Meaning that poor people spend a greater portion of any additional income than rich people do. Therefore, since a sizable percentage of banana earnings entered the hands of low income St. Lucians as opposed to sectors whose earnings were not as widely distributed, a greater portion of banana earnings was spent, and spent within the country, thus greatly stimulating the local economy.

Throughout the year 2000, the Prime Minister, Dr. Kenny D. Anthony, a law professor, not a farmer, kept repeating that the 1999 growth rate of the economy had been well above 3 percent. If so, a respectable growth rate by any standard. Yet many businesses were complaining of sluggish or stagnant growth. In that year banana export revenues were less than half its 1990 peak.

One way to explain the discrepancy between the Prime Minister's rosy economic picture and the grumbles of the business sector was that growth in other sectors of the economy, tourism, for example, was more than offsetting declines in the banana industry (hence the growth in GDP), but since as much of the earnings of the growth sectors were not remaining in the country as those of bananas and the earnings that remained weren't as widely distributed, these growth sectors weren't completely offsetting the negative effects that a declining banana industry was having on people's pocket books.

4

1993

THE STAR • APRIL 3, 1993

Farmers deserve BETTER DEAL!

Dr Ralph E. Gonsalves

The traditional cozy relationship between Geest and the banana farmers of the Windward Islands has recently come under searching re-examination. This was inevitable as the crisis in the industry unfolded, consequent upon the market changes attendant upon the establishment of the Single Europe Market and the rolling back of the preferences for Windwards bananas in the market place.

The banana farmers quite reasonably seek to gain from the roundabouts what they have lost—or expect to lose—on the swings. So they have begun to conceptualise theirs as an integrated industry and are looking for benefits from the marketing and shipping of their bananas—not merely from production.

Since Geest has been the farmers' marketers and shippers for decades, it is to be expected in the circumstances that a redefinition of the Geest-farmers relationship would be sought.

the data to support their claims: In St. Vincent and the Grenadines, Theophilus Shallow, an economist in the Central Planning Division, in a monograph entitled "The St. Vincent Banana Industry and the Single European Market," published in August 1992, showed that in 1984 farmers got 32 per cent of the green wholesale price for bananas, the Banana Growers' Association 26 per cent and Geest 42 per cent. By 1991, although the green wholesale price had risen markedly, the farmers received a mere 29 per cent thereof, the BGA 30 per cent and Geest 41 per cent.

This issue was given a full airing in the British House of Commons on November 24, 1992, by parliamentarian John Marshall (Hendon, South) in the debate on the proposed new banana regime, when he said: "An institutionalized cartel is just as evil as any other cartel. It results in much higher prices and, while the objective of the cartel is to help producers in the

1 993 began as an ominous year for St. Lucia. For it was the year that the European Community (EC) would finally transform itself into a single internal market in which member countries would abandon individual trade policies for a common approach to trade.

From the onset it was clear that with bananas the establishment of a single internal market would prove problematic because banana trade polices differed across EC members. For example, bananas from the

Windward Islands, Jamaica, Suriname and Belize, as part of their colonial legacy, were granted duty-free, unlimited access to the United Kingdom's market while imports from other sources were subjected to quotas, a licensing system and a 20 percent tariff. France, Italy, Greece, Spain and Portugal, in turn, had in place similar import licensing or bilateral import quotas to guarantee part or all of their markets for their overseas territories (OT) and African, Caribbean and Pacific countries (ACP). Belgium, Luxembourg, Denmark and Ireland employed discriminatory tariffs: they imported bananas from EC oversea territories and ACP countries duty free, and levied a 20 percent tariff on bananas from other sources—mainly Latin American countries. Finally, in contrast to all the above countries, Germany imposed no restrictions on banana imports.

The EC had conceded that in spite of its adoption of a single market protection would be given to bananas from OT and ACP countries. However, the differing banana trade policies among EC members were not only incompatible with the notion of a single market, but their inherent discrimination against Latin American bananas could be considered a violation of international trade agreements of which the EC was a party. Therefore, the possibility remained that the EC would be forced to adopt a policy of equal access, thereby bringing to an end the preferential treatment that St.

Lucia banana farmers were enjoying.

So as 1993 rolled on there was rising apprehension not only among banana farmers and the government, but among the entire population. There was justification for concern because Latin American producers had a competitive edge over other producers in the production of bananas. The evidence suggested that they produced a higher quality banana at a lower cost. For example, a 1992 Windward Islands Banana Growers' Association (WINBAN) newsletter suggested that Central America produced 26.3 tons of bananas per acre compared with the Windward Island's 5.9 tons, and their average banana bunch weighed 65 pounds compared with 30 pounds for the Windward Islands. Their competitive advantage was further evident in the fact that in Germany, the only EC country where there were no banana trade restrictions, Latin American producers accounted for 99.5 percent of the market in 1988. Moreover, despite the discriminatory tariffs that Belgium, the Netherlands, Luxembourg, Denmark and Ireland imposed on Latin American countries, in that year these countries imported 99.6 percent of their bananas from Latin America.

In view of the competitive edge that Latin American bananas enjoyed over that of the Windward Islands, the governments of these islands along with WINBAN had devoted considerable money, research and effort to improving banana quality and yield. However, they faced an uphill battle because Latin American producers enjoyed certain advantages. They had lower labor cost, their terrain and climate were better suited for banana production, and their larger scale operations facilitated better management systems and a higher degree of vertical integration.

Therefore, besides the best efforts of the Windward Islands, it was clear that under a free market arrangement their producers could not compete, and thus would lose market share. And considering the important role of the banana industry in the economic, social and political fabric of these islands, their fear was quite understandable, and proven far from groundless when in early 1993, as if taking advantage of the uncertainty and confusion surrounding the EC's soon to be announced new banana trade policy, fruit from Central America started flooding the European market, causing prices paid for Windward Islands bananas to fall from 62.2 cents per pound in 1992 to 51.3 cents in 1993. Yet, as if this wasn't enough, the pound sterling depreciated against the EC dollar from a 1991 peak of EC$5.33 to a low of EC$3.81 in February of 1993. Since banana importers in the UK paid in sterling, the exchange rate depreciation implied a fall in farmers' banana receipts. So, together, the price decline and the exchange rate depreciation caused the proceeds that St. Lucian banana farmers received from the SLBGA to fall to a low of 26 cents per pound, a return considered below most farmers' costs of production.

Farmers could well understand that the happenings in Europe were beyond their control, and beyond the control of their banana association. However, It seemed that their problems didn't stop with the realities of the European market. The SLBGA had chosen no other time but this period of falling prices to tighten farm credit, and to increase cess deductions for inputs farmers had purchased on credit. To top all these, there were reports that the SLBGA was wasteful, inefficient and corrupt. These reports suggested that the association was spending $10,000 per month on attending meetings. To collect their $200 per meeting, some directors attended meetings that weren't required, and on certain days some attended several meetings, getting paid for each meeting. One director even claimed the $200 for representing the association at a cocktail party. There were also reports that directors were taking unnecessary overseas trips at the association's expense, and that there was nepotism in staff promotions, especially in senior management positions. For example, it was alleged that someone was given the post of executive secretary to the association simply because he had campaigned for the appointment of some directors.

Farmers had no control over the happenings in

Europe, but they could surely have a say in how their banana association functioned. After all, were they not the owners of the association?

So by May 1993, activist farmers led by Patrick Joseph and Abel Wilson, an ex-director of the board of directors of the SLBGA, organized themselves into the Banana Salvation Committee (BSC), the vehicle by which they hoped to start taking their future into their own hands.

The BSC demanded a guaranteed minimum price of 30 cents per pound of bananas, the dissolution of the Board of Directors, the appointment of a new board, and the streamlining of SLBGA operations to return a larger portion of banana revenues to farmers. If these demands weren't met, the BSC threatened to call a banana strike.

No one. Not the government, not the Civil Service Association, not the Teachers Union, not the St. Lucia Workers Union, not the Vieux Fort General and Dock Workers Union, not the Chamber of Commerce, not the Prime Minister, himself a banana farmer, not the SLBGA, not the Windward Islands Banana Growers' Association, not Geest Industries, not the population, was willing to meet farmers' demands, so on October 5, 1993, with their industry, their very livelihood seemingly falling apart, farmers ignored history and went on the strike that would end with the death of two of their members.

Deaths that not only shocked the nation but marked the beginning of the transformation of the banana industry in St. Lucia.

5

The Rape Of Eden

Now, if farmers had asked historians for advise, they would have been informed that by attempting to decide their own fate they were swimming against the current of history. Because ever since Columbus appeared on the Caribbean scene, the fate of St. Lucia and the other picturesque islands punctuating the Caribbean Sea and separating it from the Atlantic Ocean, had been almost totally dependent on outsiders and events taking place thousands of miles away.

The Kalinagos, better known as the Caribs, were the first to come to grips with this reality. Certainly, they had thought of themselves as masters of not only their own fate, but that of the Caribbean. After all, hadn't they wiped out or chased away the Awaraks from whichever island they, the Caribs, had chosen to grace with their presence? But what the Caribs could not have anticipated, what they hadn't bargained for, much less fathom, was the extent of European greed. Of course, being the ferocious warriors that they were, they had put up a valiant fight to maintain hold of the notion that, yes, they were masters of their own fate. But with only bows and arrows as defense against a relentless European greed backed by iron and steel, guns and gun powder, and old world religion and germs, the fate of the Caribs was a foregone conclusion long before even the first angry arrow left its bow, or the sound of the first gunfire shattered forever the peace of the islands.

Three times the Caribs wiped out or drove away the English. First in 1605, then in 1640, and then again in 1663, but they soon bowed to the inevitable when they sold St. Lucia to the English (residing in Barbados). So today the legacy of the once ferocious and arrogant Caribs has been reduced to the making of dugout fishing pirouges; the craft of making clay pots; the farming and processing of cassava for food; Hewanorra, the name of the international airport, derived from Iouanalao, the

Carib name for the island, meaning "there where the iguana is found," the village of Canaries, named after the Carib name for clay pots; and a small minority of Carib descendants (mixed with other races, mainly African and European) concentrated in the southwest (Choiseul in particular) of the island.

With the Caribs out of the way, the fate of St. Lucia was mostly decided by what was happening in Europe. Quarrels originating there between the French and English played themselves out in the West Indies in much the same way the cold war between America and the Soviet Union was waged in the Third World. And nowhere else in the West Indies was this more true than in St. Lucia. Nowhere else was there a better example of European greed gone berserk. Fourteen times the island changed hands between the English and French. For a long time this constant fighting, colonial interchanging, and instability didn't only retard the building of schools, infrastructure, and administrative institutions, but made the island a haven for deserters, smugglers and people fleeing from bankruptcy. Thus, throughout the 19th and early 20th century, St. Lucia remained one of the poorest islands of the West Indies. Castries, then called Carènage, was little more than a vermin and mosquito invested swamp, causing frequent outbreaks of yellow fever, which, for example, claimed 121 lives in the later half of 1763.

On the other hand, each outbreak of war presented the enslaved Africans an opportunity to revolt and escape into the mountains. The most famous of these slave revolts began in 1794, the same year the English had again wrested the island from the French who, only a few months before, on the heels of the French Revolution, had freed the slaves so that they could join the fight against the British. Upon repossession, the English had promptly re-established slavery. The ex-slaves, suddenly finding themselves once again in bondage, took to the forests where, along with French Revolutionaries, they launched a guerilla war against the British and white plantation owners that lasted well into 1796. By the time the guerilla fighters surrendered, they had destroyed seven-eighths of the plantations, ransacked and burnt to the ground many towns and villages, and, according to one account, had killed eighty-five (mostly white) families.

Today the legacy of the runaway slaves comes to us in the legend of *Neg Mawons*, runaway niggers, a term in St. Lucian idiom that means ignorant, savage, and backward. Engulfed by virgin forests and nearly unscalable mountains, many *Neg Mawons* remained free right into emancipation. Failing to defeat them, the plantation owners resorted to the next best thing. They degraded and dehumanized them, and, unfortunately, given today's connotation of *Neg Mawon*, this European propaganda still lingers in the island's psyche.

The rivalry over the island had consequences beyond economics. Up to 1803 when England finally gained lasting control of St. Lucia, the French had occupied the island ninety years to the English twenty. So today, while the country follows a British system of government, it has a French civil code. The official language is English, but French patois is the native tongue, and most of the names of the towns, villages and landmarks are French. While the country follows a British system of education, more than 80 percent of the population is Roman Catholic, as opposed to Anglican or Protestant, and up to the 1970's the Roman Catholic Church controlled most of the schools. In fact, just removing the schools from the control of the nuns and priests had proven to be a struggle. And up to 2002 and beyond, there were still primary schools on the island where the school day began with a recitation of the Catechism.

Sugar came to St. Lucia in 1763 and ushered a new era in the island's history, for with sugar St. Lucia became a full-blown plantation economy in which large tracts of cheaply acquired land was combined with enslaved African labor to produce sugar for export to England. And since the plantations and therefore the island produced little else but sugar and one or two other cash crops, England supplied most of the island's necessities and manufactured goods. Hence the island never had a chance to be anything else than a supplier of raw materials.

By 1777, just fourteen years after sugar was introduced, the land area under cultivation increased to one-sixth of the total, estates doubled from 400 to 804, functioning administrative quarters doubled from four to nine, and the population of enslaved Africans tripled from about 5,000 to 16,000.

Before this European encounter, the Africans and the many others that followed probably never doubted that they were masters of their own fate. Little did they know that their whole existence was suddenly about to change because their northern neighbors had developed a sweet tooth.

There they were, in Africa, in the middle of their daily activities, when suddenly they were snatched, yoked into chain gangs, marched to the coast, stock-piled into slave holding dungeons to await shipment, and then packed into the cargo holds of ships for the transatlantic voyage. Those who survived the march to the African coast, and those who survived the slave holding dungeons, and those who survived the transatlantic voyage, arrived weak, dazed and sickly on some Caribbean shore, were auctioned to the highest bidder, and marched to one sugar plantation or another. Awaking the following morning in a world they had never imagined existed, they were thrown together with other Africans of different tribes, of different customs, speaking different languages, and assigned to sugar fields, where on minimal rations of food and clothing they would labor for the rest of their lives, six days a week, from dust to dawn, whipped, maimed, killed even, for any show of resistance. Any show of rebellion against the notion that someone else dictated every aspect of their lives—when and whom they could wed, where they could go, what aspects of their African culture they could practice, what time they had to awake, what time they had to go to bed.

Faced with these conditions, conditions designed to strip them of their humanity, to survive both physically and spiritually the enslaved Africans had to find ways of reaffirming their humanity; ways of continuing their religion; ways of reconstructing their sense of community; ways of celebrating the passages of birth, marriage, and death; ways of overtly or covertly resisting their enslavement; ways of getting around their oppressors' attempts at stamping out all aspects of their African culture that they considered threatening to the status quo; ways of communicating with their fellow Africans who spoke a language different from their own, and of communicating or discommunicating (when it suited their purposes) with their oppressors; if nothing else, ways of convincing themselves that, yes, they still had some control, no matter how little, over their fate.

So in St. Lucia, to communicate among themselves and with the plantation owners, the enslaved Africans employed the vocabulary of their French oppressors but the syntax and cadence of their African languages to form a new and different language that we now call Kwéyòl. During slavery and right into modern times, this same Kwéyòl that the slaves had forged out of necessity, and today is celebrated as Jouné Kwéyòl and has become a source of national pride, national identity, one of the things that distinguishes St. Lucian culture from all other cultures, was regarded as slave language, vulgar, suited only for the ignorant and uneducated.

The beat of the African drum (one of the few visible African traditions that remained intact under slavery), with which the slaves kept their African spirit alive, the glue that bonded them into a living, breathing community (since this was the one language that Africans of all tribes, nationalities, and languages understood), which, along with its associated dances, the plantation owners regarded as vulgar, licentious, primitive, now pulsates in reggae, calypso and cadence. In much the same manner that African rhythms have given way to blues, soul and jazz in America, and samba in Brazil.

To the plantation owners the slaves were an investment no different from the plantation livestock, or the machinery used to process the sugarcane. Their objective was to gain maximum profit from the labors of the slaves, while spending the least amount on their welfare. As the least costly means of feeding the slaves, they brought in breadfruit, plantains, bananas and other high energy yielding plants, and from the American colonies they imported salted cod (saltfish).

Under those circumstances, again trying to take some control over their lives, the slaves had to come up with ingenious ways to get any kind of variety in their diet, or, for that matter, just to get enough to eat. They put to good use the cows' feet, pigs' feet, animal blood and entrails that the plantations would otherwise throw away. Thus today the salted cod, once considered slave food, that the slaves probably abhorred, has become the country's national dish in the form of saltfish and green figs (bananas). The cow feet, pig feet, animal blood and entrails have become national delicacies as souse and black pudding.

Arguably, no other group of slaves did more to perpetuate the island's African culture than the runaway slaves, the Neg Mawons. This proposition suggests itself for several reasons. Firstly, evidence suggests that the slaves who were most likely to runaway were not those born in slavery, but those who had had a taste of freedom. Most of those would have been born and raised in Africa, and therefore would have most of their African culture intact, a culture to pass on from one generation to another. Secondly, the concept of self-selectivity suggests that the slaves who chose to run away were those who were the most proud, the most independent, the most obstinate. The very ones who were most likely to resist the efforts of the plantations to strip them of their African culture. Thirdly, away from the plantation, not only were the *Neg Mawons* less influenced by the de-Africanizing slave culture that the plantation system bred but they were more free to perpetuate their own African way of life. Thus, although today the term *Neg Mawon* has come to signify ignorant, savage, backward, the island probably owes a lot to the *Neg Mawons* for the survival of its African culture.

6

In the Beginning

Even the establishment of the banana industry, the economic activity from which the island had drawn so much of its sustenance, had more to do with the needs of Great Britain than the demands of the island's inhabitants. Up to 1950, bananas produced in Jamaica and shipped and marketed by Fyffes, a subsidiary of the American owned United Fruit Company, dominated the United Kingdom market, capturing, for example, more than 86 percent of the market in 1937. Banana imports were banned from the United Kingdom during World War II, but when imports resumed in 1946, banana production in Jamaica was only one-fifth of its 1938 peak, creating a shortage on the United Kingdom market. Taking advantage of the shortage, British owned Antilles Products Ltd. established banana operations in the Windward Islands and signed a 15-year contract to buy and ship all of the islands' exportable quality fruit.

This wasn't the first time that attempts had been made to establish bananas in St. Lucia. A previous attempt in 1925 by the Swift Banana Company, a subsidiary of United Fruit, was forced to go out of business after the disease called Panama devastated the industry. This time around, bananas had an ally. For some time now Britain had been concerned about the near monopoly that bananas grown or shipped by the United Fruit Company had on the United Kingdom market. This monopoly exacerbated the persistent trade and balance of payments deficit that the United Kingdom was then experiencing, and made it more difficult to pay back war debts owed to the United States of America. Therefore, viewing a Windward Islands banana industry as a means of breaking this monopoly, Britain didn't only welcome the move but actively supported it with the granting of preferential treatment to all Commonwealth bananas.

There was a second reason why Britain sanctioned the move. The depression years of the 1930's and 1940's was a period of extreme and deplorable poverty in not only St. Lucia but the whole Caribbean. A state of affairs that was causing considerable unrest and discontent in the British colonies. So besides addressing its own trade and fiscal concerns, Britain hoped that a viable Windward Islands banana industry would help alleviate poverty and unrest in the region, and help lessen its share of the islands' economic burden.

British support was essential for bananas to take root in the Windward Islands, but the second factor that led to the success of the industry fell in place when in 1953 Antilles Products Ltd. sold their Windward Islands banana interest to British owned Geest Industries who in turn won exclusive rights to ship and market all the bananas that the Windward Islands could produce. As a marketing and shipping company with an extensive dis-tribution network for fruits and flowers, Geest

Industries was ideally suited for leveraging Windward Islands bananas. So with a failing sugar industry, a company that could do justice to the marketing of Windward Islands bananas, and a British government with a personal stake in the success of the enterprise, all what was needed for bananas to take off was for the Windward Islands to put in place structures that would facilitate the production and export of the fruit.

Meeting the challenge, the island played its part, when, by 1953, with the encouragement of Geest and the United Kingdom, St. Lucian banana farmers, like those of the other Windward Islands, were organized into a banana growers' association, which, through 1964 and 1967 legislation, was made a statutory institution, operating much like a government agency or ministry. The association was run by a board of directors comprising government appointees and elected farmers, with the stipulation that elected members of the House of Assembly could not serve on the board. Operating much like national cooperatives, the banana growers' associations (one in each of the Windward Islands) were responsible for purchasing all export quality bananas from farmers, and packaging, delivering and selling the bananas to Geest. In addition, the St. Lucia Banana Growers' Association controlled diseases affecting bananas, and through banana extension services provided farmers technical advise on improved agronomic practices.

Additional structure came in 1958 when the governments of the Windward Islands, along with their banana growers' associations, established the Windward Islands Banana Growers' Association (WINBAN), which served as the umbrella organization to negotiate and monitor marketing and shipping contracts for bananas, to represent the growers on the United Kingdom Banana Trade Advisory Committee, to initiate research and to supply farmers with technical assistance and banana inputs. Six years later, in 1964, WINBAN established its main research center in St. Lucia's Roseau Valley. The center was officially opened by a no lesser personage than the Queen of England, giving testament to the importance Britain placed on Windward Islands bananas.

With the inception of WINBAN, the full structure, the structure that banana farmers would strike against in 1993, to move bananas from the remotest interior of the Windward Islands to the fruit baskets of British housewives, fell in place. The Banana Growers' Associations (BGA) purchased from farmers all export quality bananas that they could grow. Geest in turn bought all the exportable bananas that the BGAs had for sale. Once a week Geest loaded its ships with Windward Islands bananas destined for England. In the United Kingdom Geest sold some of the bananas green to wholesalers at a wholesale price termed the green market price (GMP), and the remaining fruit went to Geest ripening facilities, which was then sold to retailers at a retail price called the "ripe price."

From these two prices, Geest calculated a weighted average price called the green wholesale price (GWP). Out of this GWP the company deducted charges for receiving, loading and shipping, and for cost incurred in the distribution, handling and marketing of the fruit. The balance of the green wholesale price after those deductions was paid to the banana associations as the export price. The banana associations in turn deducted from that export price all their expenses, which included administration expenses, cost of banana packaging materials, and cost of banana inputs such as fertilizer and pesticides. Finally, what was left of the green wholesale price after Geest's and the associations' deductions were paid to farmers as the growers' price.

What this suggests is that no matter the condition of the market for bananas—falling prices, exchange rate fluctuations, fluctuating demand and supply—both Geest and the BGAs were virtually ensured of covering their costs. Farmers were the only ones who bore the risk and uncertainty surrounding demand and supply. This was why it was quite understandable, especially in the face of falling prices, that farmers would revolt against this system as they did on October 5, 1993 when they went on a banana strike to protest against corruption in their banana association and a grower price below their cost of production.

7

Grant It to Us God!

Emancipation came in 1838 but the task of the island's black population of freeing themselves from servitude was far from over. The plantation system depended on a large pool of low-waged, unskilled labor, and during slavery the plantations controlled all aspects of the lives of their workers even to the extent of setting rules on how workers could relate or interact with each other. So, in a sense, the plantation system, which emancipation left intact, was the instrument by which slavery was executed.

Naturally, though slavery was over, plantation owners expected to continue enjoying large pools of black labor over whom they had complete control, and to whom they only needed to pay token wages. By 1838, sugar in St. Lucia and the British West Indies was in decline. Planters were debt-ridden, and because of competition from European beet sugar and slave-grown cane sugar from Cuba and Brazil, sugar prices and profits were falling. So with their very survival at stake and an unwillingness to pay much for what they once had for free, white planters sought ways to keep the black population latched to their plantations and be totally dependent on them for their existence. Accordingly, they imposed new house taxes for education and roads that discouraged workers from leaving the plantations; they opposed regulations that would grant crown lands to ex-slaves, and they forced the ex-slaves who refused to remain full-time in their employment to either pay rent or vacate the huts and plots of land that they had occupied rent-free during slavery.

Fortunately for the ex-slaves, unlike islands like Barbados, Antigua, St. Kitts and Nevis, at the time of emancipation St. Lucia had an ample supply of unclaimed, arable land. The relatively late arrival of sugarcane and the century of rivalry between the English and the French had retarded the island's settlement. And more land became available when, in response to declining fortunes in sugar, some plantations folded and some others reduced the size of their land holdings. However, even if the island had been more extensively cultivated, the mountains that had given refuge to the *Neg Mawons* and which were unsuited for sugarcane or plantation agriculture would have ensured that the plantations left untouched large tracts of land that were suited for small scale cultivation.

The availability of land undermined the white planters' efforts to curtail the freedom and autonomy of the black population, and understandably the black population was more than eager to put distance between themselves and plantation life. After all, to them plantation life was slavery and slavery was plantation life.

During slavery, and especially during the four years of apprenticeship leading to emancipation, the slaves were allowed provision plots on which in their spare time they grew food to supplement their slave rations. Since whatever they produced on these plots was theirs to keep and dispose of as they wished, a local market had developed where those who grew more than they could consume sold or traded their surpluses. So with emancipation many of them sought their own land to extend the notion of growing their own food for sale at the market and to feed themselves. Some who had

money saved from these market activities bought sur-
plus plantation lands from their previous masters; some
left the plantations and the coast and established home-
steads in the mountainous interior of the island on the
same lands the plantations had pronounced as marginal,
unfit for sugarcane; some occupied abandoned plantation lands; others simply squatted on crown lands. Even
those who stayed on with the plantations were only willing to work just so many hours and then devote the rest
of their time to their own plots of land.

There were others who wanted to put more than just
distance between themselves and plantation life. They
wished to leave farming altogether. The very act of tilling
the soil was to them an act of slavery. Instead of working
the plantations or farming their own land, they turned to
fishing, cutting logwood, making coals, and shop-keep-
ing.

The formation of the black population into independent households, independent economic units, instead of
being just extensions of the plantations as existed under
slavery, increased demand for a variety of goods and
services. Soon these rising needs allowed some of the
black population who had acquired definite skills and
trades during slavery to establish themselves, at least
part-time, as independent blacksmiths, seamstresses,
tailors, masons, carpenters, joiners, and other such
trades. Before emancipation the plantations were

responsible for just about all economic life on the island, but with freedom the black population was starting to generate economic activities independent of the plantations.

With so many ex-slaves eager to make it on their own, in spite of the white planters' best efforts, it was difficult for them to find sufficient labor to work their plantations, at least not at the wages they were willing to pay. Desperate to keep their wage cost low in the face of falling sugar prices and yet grow enough cane to keep their sugar mills running, some plantations entered into a share cropping arrangement called the métairie system. Under this system, in place of wages, the plantations paid workers either a share of the sugar crop or a share of the proceeds. The métairie system soon fell into disfavor, however, because as sugar prices continued to fall workers increasingly found themselves at the losing end of the arrangement.

Soon, partly in response to the labor shortage and partly to offset the overwhelmingly black population of the island, the plantation owners attempted to recruit European workers. But disease, death, and an unwillingness to do work once set aside for slaves, *negs* (niggers), made many of the few white recruits the plantation owners were able to obtain of little use. Then, spoilt by years of slave labor, black labor, the plantations went back to Africa, although this time for recruits and not slaves. But the Africans, having barely missed the slave ships, were no more eager to cross the Atlantic Ocean on promises of a better life than were their shackled predecessors. Less than 300 came and most of them settled at Micoud, Gros Islet, Sarot, Guinee, Fond Assau and Dannezan. This left the Indian subcontinent, colonized by the same masters of the owners of the sugar plantations, as the defacto source of cheap labor. Between 1837 and 1895 more than 4,300 East Indians arrived on the island. Of those, 643 came in 1893 on the emigrant ship *Volga* when it was shipwrecked at Vigie Point. Luckily, all the passengers were rescued.

The East Indians, not to be mistaken with the Caribs who had long since been reduced to a footnote in St. Lucian history, came not as slaves, but as indentured servants. On promises of return passages, they agreed to give five to ten years of labor to the plantations at daily wages (in the 1840s) of one shilling for men, eightpence for women and four pence for children.

The Indians came thinking that they were in control of their lives. After all, unlike the Africans, they didn't arrive in chains, and most came of their own free will. But little did they know that slave or not they weren't masters of their own fate. They were not slaves, but often the conditions under which they lived were not far different from slavery. The plantations sought to exercise over their indentured servants the same total control that they had over their slaves. For the first few months before the Indians had established their provision plots, the plantations took a third of their wages for food rations that were no different from what the slaves used to receive. The Indians' contracts called for seven or eight-hour workdays, but very often they were forced to work ten, to twelve hours, and any fewer hours incurred cuts in pay. Accused of laziness, they were sometimes beaten, their week's wages forfeited, and their family plots withdrawn. The estates were supposed to supply them with free housing and medical attention, but the houses they received were the same thatched huts the slaves once occupied and usually they saw a doctor only when they were dying, when it was too late. On top of all that, at the end of the Indians' five or ten years of indentureship, the white planters would often renege on their promises of free passages back to India.

The Indians were treated not much better than the slaves, but they were never slaves, they were never shackled, so naturally they considered themselves perhaps lower than the white planters, but definitely above the black population. Not only were they never slaves, but they had arrived with more of their distinctiveness, more of their culture intact than the Africans who had arrived in shackles. And they aimed to keep it that way. Drawing from their caste system, they tried hard to avoid what to them was contaminating themselves with ex-slaves. They isolated themselves in village pockets with names like Fond Coolie, Augier, and Piero. Visits from their ministers residing in Trinidad helped them hold on fast to their Hindu and Islamic religions. But surrounded by a sea of black people espousing a different culture, and Roman Catholic priests and Protestant ministries who regarded Hindu and Islam as pagan religions, the Indians were fighting a losing battle. The Presbyterian Church of Canada opened not only Indian ministries but also small schools in several rural districts, and when these schools disappeared by 1900, Roman Catholic schools took their places. Before long, especially after 1880 when their ministers from Trinidad stopped visiting, the Indians were largely converted to Catholicism and, to a lesser extent, the Protestant faiths.

For their part, Blacks looked upon the Indians with scorn. They may have been slaves, but they were not indentured, they were no longer in bondage. They thought the Indians were subjecting themselves too willingly to the slave conditions that they, the Black population, had so recently escaped. The Indians were helping to bring back slavery. They were trespassers who were conniving with the white planters against the Black population. After all, the influx of Indian emigrants was partly responsible for keeping plantation wages down.

As in some of the territories (Guyana for example)

where East Indians were brought in, a classic confrontation developed between Indians and Blacks. But unlike Guyana, where the Indian population was half or more than half the population, St. Lucia was able to avoid any violent racial clashes. The Indian population, which was more or less seconded in village pockets, was never more than one-eighth of the island's inhabitants and up to the year 2002 they formed less than 3 percent of the population. Because of the overwhelming number of Blacks to Indians, confrontations in St. Lucia never amounted to more than social scuffles, the calling of names and the Indians keeping to themselves.

Since then much has changed. There are many more intermarriages between Blacks and Indians, Blacks are living in most, if not all, the Indian villages. The Indians are much more wide-spread, and are an integral part of the broad society. So much so that it would be misleading to talk of an Indian culture versus a Black culture. Like the rest of the population, few Indians can speak Hindi, and Hindu and Islam are virtually nonexistent. There is now just a St. Lucian culture, a St. Lucian people.

Curried meats, roti, dalpouri, and other dishes or methods of cooking that the Indians brought over are no longer thought of as Indian cooking or Indian foods, but as St. Lucian or West Indian cuisine. Kwéyòl, saltfish and green figs, souse, black pudding, developed during slavery, belong as much to the Indians who were never enslaved as they do to the descendants of the enslaved Africans. So to the cultural mix (of African, European and a sprinkle of Carib) forged under the crucible of slavery and the plantation system, was added East Indian culture to form what is regarded today as St. Lucian culture.

8

Gods of The Land

Once proper structures were in place to move bananas from the deepest interior of St. Lucia to British supermarkets, farmers took to bananas as if the fruit was manna from heaven. But what they couldn't have known was that the banana was not only a jealous god, but a very sensitive and particular one. In 1925, when the people, its subjects, first attempted to establish the fruit on the island, they had let size and physical appearances fool them. Consequently, they had paid homage to Gros Michel which stood as tall as twenty-two feet, produced bunches weighing more than a hundred pounds, with fingers almost the size of plantains, and as smooth as velvet, and whose ripened flesh literally melted in ones mouth. Falling prey to all those appealing, jezebel-like qualities, like a man charmed by a harlot, the people had chosen no other banana variety to pay homage to than Gros Michel. Greatly displeased, because this wasn't the form in which it wanted to be praised, god deliberately allowed a disease called Panama to wipe out Gros Michel, bringing an end to the banana industry before it had even begun.

So, like the children of Israel wandering forty years in the wilderness, it would take another twenty-five years, in 1950, before another attempt was made to cultivate bananas commercially. This time around the people had learnt their lesson. They had ignored appearances, and complying with the wishes of god, they paid homage to Cavendish instead of Gros Michel. Compared with Gros Michel, Cavendish was more blunt, less brightly colored, had less stature, and its bunches and fingers were somewhat smaller. Altogether, it wasn't as visually appealing as Gros Michel. But the plant was resistant to the disease called Panama, and its deeper root system and shorter frame made it less susceptible to strong winds and hurricanes. God was appeased, so it was then and only then that the banana industry was destined to take off.

Still, being a jealous god, the banana could not entertain any other gods besides himself, so it went to battle with sugar, the evil god that had enslaved or indentured the people and had dominated the land for two centuries. Now, to be honest, by then sugar was a tired and sick god, paying in full measure for the great evil it had brought upon the people and the land. The abolition of slavery, which led to a shortage of cheap labor; competition from cheaper, slave-grown sugar from Cuba and Brazil; competition from protected and subsidized European beet sugar; and the continued use of outdated and inefficient processing methods; all contributed to the sickness of the sugar industry. Unfortunately for the people and the land, the same people whom sugar had enslaved or indentured, since sugar was by far the main economic activity and source of employment, its decline brought great misery and poverty.

Nonetheless, being the evil god that it was, sugar fought desperately to maintain its hold on the land. The god played many tricks on the ex-slaves to keep them working on the plantation for mere pittance. It imposed new house taxes for education and roads, it opposed regulation that would grant government lands to the people, and it forced the people who refused to remain full-time in its employment either to pay rent or vacate the huts and plots of land that they had occupied for free during slavery. Worse, the evil god tricked the people into a métairie system whereby they would receive a percentage of the sugar crop or a share of the proceeds as payment. When none of those things worked, it went all over the world—Europe, Africa, Asia—in search of cheap labor to replace the slave labor it once had for free. But no matter what it tried to stay alive, the writing was on the wall! All that was missing for the evil god's final demise was for the banana god to assert itself, and once the people had paid proper homage by worshiping the banana god in its proper form, it was more than ready, willing, and able to displace sugar. So after many strikes by sugar workers during which they were beaten, shot and jailed, sugar left the island in 1962 for good.

With sugar gone the people sang praises to the banana god. But what they didn't realize was that, unlike manna from heaven, the banana was a task master, and that the unmistakable dark-brown stains with which it covered its subjects' clothing, pronouncing them his for life, weren't the only sacrifice that it demanded of them.

In abject obedience, farmers across the length and breadth of the island picked up their cutlasses, forks, crowbars, and pickaxes, went to every nook and cranny on the island, where only footpaths led, to wage war for the banana. They transformed virgin forest into burnt bare land, and then with their crowbars, pickaxes and forks they tore open the burnt, bare soil, pried out boulders and cut through roots of trees as hard as rocks, and systematically punctured the land with holes eight feet apart, twelve to eighteen inches deep, and twenty-four inches wide. They dug networks of gutters to allow excessive rain water to drain into the streams flowing at the bottom of hills or in the middle of valleys, instead of water logging the land, drowning the banana plants and providing a medium for plant diseases to fester. For plant material farmers selected healthy offshoots (suckers they are called) of plants from established fields. But before planting these, they had carefully to trim off the portion of the corm infected with nematodes and borer weevils and as an additional precaution against nematodes they sprinkled the planting hole with a granular nematicide.

That was just the beginning. Three to six times during the course of the year, farmers carried fifty and hundred-pound bags of fertilizer downhill, uphill, across rivers and on to their farms. Then they filled buckets that once held butter with the fertilizer pellets, and with dry coconut shells or small tin cans as scoops, they applied a quarter to three-quarter pound of fertilizer around each banana plant, not too close for the fertilizer to burn the roots, yet not too far for the rain to carry the fertilizer away from the plant.

With rain and fertilizer the weeds flourished. So with cutlasses as weapons, farmers fought year-round, uphill battles against the weeds. The emergence of gramoxone and other herbicides brought some relief. With gramoxone, for example, the weeds burnt brown and then withered. But gramoxone killed more than just the tissue of the weeds. It killed their very spirits. Pulled up by hand or cut off with a cutlass, the weeds grew back quickly. But with gramoxone the weeds took months to reappear. It was as if the gramoxone entered the soil and forever changed the conditions that allowed the weeds to thrive. The disappearance of the toads, some the size of breadfruits, that once claimed the farms as their kingdoms, the fer-de-lances that used to be a menace to Praslin farmers, and the large fishes that once inhabited the deeper stone-free parts of the rivers—sacrifices to god—could attest to the effectiveness of farm chemicals like gramoxone.

Never mind the highbrow fussiness of the banana. It presents itself as a tree but a herb it is. And as a herb it is very fragile. Its roots are shallow and, unlike tree crops, it has no tap root. Strong wind, running water (digging into the roots) or root diseases can easily topple the plant. So when the banana is young it wants farmers to treat it as tenderly as they would a baby, and when bearing fruit, it commands the farmers to treat it as carefully as they would a pregnant woman. Farmers had to be constantly pruning off unwanted suckers, dry leaves and dead bark material from the banana plants to avoid the harmful viruses, bacteria, and funguses (such as cucumber mosaic, moka disease, and leaf spot), any of which could seriously undermine the growth of the plant.

When borer weevils start to eat the banana's corm and root system, farmers had to apply primicid, and when parasitic nematodes took their turn, farmers had no choice but to seek the assistance of nematicides with names like furadan, mocap, nemacur, miral, rugby, and vydate.

When the banana has flowered and the flower develops into green hands, the banana gains knowledge of good and evil, and it starts to complain. "Why leave me so naked? Flower thrips, rust thrips, aphids and weevils are scarring my fruit, spoiling my beauty." Again farmers obliged. They broke off the male flowers and false hands hanging at the end of the banana stems, removed the black appendages or nails attached to the end of the banana fingers, and clothed the banana bunches in chemical (dursban) impregnated blue nylon dresses (diothene tube).

When deep in labor with roots and corm undermined by nematodes and borer weevils, the banana realizes that it is easy prey to heavy wind and rain and thus demands of the farmer to prop it. Again farmers yielded to god. They braced each such banana plant with bamboo poles or with double-string (polypropylene twine) props pulling in the opposite direction of the potential fall.

But their work was far from done. Initially, the island shipped the banana to England without any clothes. But the banana didn't like this arrangement at all. It arrived bruised, ashamed of its nakedness, and unprotected from the English winter. So the banana demanded to be clothed and looking its best when it arrived at Buckingham Palace. So starting in 1956, to please god, farmers wrapped the banana bunches in sheets of paper (lined with a soft, fluffy, tissue paper-like bedding called *kakan*) kept in place with twines tied around the mid section of the bunches. Then they slipped on nylon dresses over the bunches and then taped the ends of the nylon dresses onto the ends of the stems.

To protect the banana against bruises, farmers used the dry leaves of the bananas as padding between layers of banana bunches. But after a while the banana decided that banana straws were not good enough for it; they were coarse and ugly and made the god look bad. So sponge soon replaced the straws that once littered the countryside and the shipping points of Vieux Fort and Castries on banana days. Instead of straw cushions, there were thick sponge mats; instead of straw lining banana trays and interleaving layers of banana bunches, there were small sheets of sponge.

Yet satisfied, the banana complained that it no longer wanted to be shipped in whole bunches. Obliging, in 1970 its stewards began to dehandle the bunches and ship the hands in boxes. This change revolutionized the industry. Safe and secure in boxes, the banana no longer needed the protective sponges. So the sponges went the way of the banana straws. Buying points also disappeared, giving way to boxing plants: large two-story structures, where the top floors were used for storage and for stapling banana boxes. But the real action was on the ground floor where banana bunches coming from the farm were dehandled, the desirable hands placed in plastic trays for weighing and then washed in a pool of water. They were then transferred to an adjacent pool filled with a fungicide solution that provided protection against the bacteria called crown rot. Next the hands were placed on conveyor belts that carried them to the back of the plant for packing into boxes.

Before boxes, the loading of bananas unto the banana boat was an incredible sight. Hundreds of women with tightly wound waists, and wearing for head gear a cloth pad secured with a lace tied under their chins scurried like ants to the galvanized banana shed where men standing ready loaded banana bunches onto the women's heads. Then, as if the shed had caught fire, the women rushed out from under the shed toward the opened windows on the side of the banana boat. Once there, men standing at these windows that were like the mouths of caves, snatched the bananas from the women's heads and passed them onto the next man in line, who in turn passed them to the next man in line, and so on, until the bananas were deposited deep into the refrigerated bosom of the boat. The women did not stay to watch the completion of the relay they had started. Even before the men had snatched the bananas from their heads they hurried back to pick up another bunch. Into the wee hours of the morning, non-stop, these women, like bats, darted back and forth between the banana boat and the banana shed. There was no time to waste; their pay depended on how many bunches they carried for the night. One watched in amazement and awe as thousands of stems disappeared from the banana shed; as barebacked men, bathed in perspiration, and muscles straining and bulging, passed thousands of bunches to the man next in line, in nonstop action.

With the boxing of the fruit, the loading of bananas onto the banana boat became no more the beehive of activity it once was. A few men unloaded boxes packed with bananas from trucks and stacked them onto wooden pallets. On loading day cranes lifted the loaded pallets onto the banana boat.

After all those changes, the banana was still dissatisfied; it complained that it passes through too many hands. Further, it suggested that why not dehandle and box me right under the plant from which I came, instead of carrying me miles to a boxing plant during which I get bruised and hurt? After all, look at all the rejects this is causing. Again, since the banana was god, its wish was farmers' command. So requested, so done. Farmers dehandled the banana bunch right in their fields, drained the hands of latex, then to prevent the hands from rotting caused by crown rot, they initially applied a fungicide-impregnated pad (a WINBAN patented invention) to where the hand was severed from the stem, but later rather than applying crown pads they simply bathed the hands in a basin of fungicide solution. So treated, the hands were then boxed.

With each farmer boxing his or her own bananas right under the banana plants, boxing plants, like the buying points before them, became obsolete. They became relics of the past, monuments to the banana god. No longer do farmers gather at these factories of god to share jokes, share their mistrust of government, complain about banana prices and meet the opposite sex. The era when the banana harvest was as much social as economic, when the buying points and boxing plants were the factories and town halls of rural communities, had ended.

So in view of all what farmers had had to endure, one could well understand their frustration and anger, when in 1993 no one heeded their call for the banana god to uphold its share of the bargain and provide them a decent living. After all, paying homage to god wasn't even half of what farmers had had to undergo. Besides diseases, insects, and uncertain prices, they had to be forever concerned about the elements.

In 1960 Hurricane Abby devastated the banana industry; in 1967 Hurricane Beulah destroyed 75 percent of the banana crop; between 1970 and 1977, taking over where Hurricane Beulah left off, severe droughts brought the banana industry to its knees; in 1979 Hurricane David poured its share of misery on banana farmers, and not to be out done, in 1980 Hurricane Allen reduced the banana crop to nought. All this farmers had had to put up with, so when god, Geest Industries, WINBAN, the SLBGA, and the Prime Minister, himself a banana farmer, hence a servant of god, had forsaken them, it was quite understandable, predictable even, that they would go on strike. What was impossible to forecast, however, was that the strike would end with deaths in the valley.

9

The Struggle for Survival

However sweet and exhilarating was emancipation, the struggles of the black population were far from over. True, under the euphoria of freedom they had rushed to sever ties with the plantations. But the reality of white planters owning most of the island's productive assets, including the best lands and the sugar mills, was inescapable. In fact, white planters controlled not just the economy but also the political machinery. Then the island had a crown colony government with an administrator presiding over an Executive and a Legislative Council. The Executive Council was comprised mainly of officiated members, while the Legislative Council included, along with members of the Executive Council, a chief justice and five of the principal proprietors (mainly plantation owners) of the island. The Executive Council, which controlled the finances, levied taxes, and authorized public expenditures, had far greater powers than its legislative counterpart. Nonetheless, both Councils were the exclusive domain of the white establishment and virtually no nonwhites could serve.

True, the black population had its freedom and was the overwhelming majority, but in reality the island belonged not to them but to the white establishment, and it was administered primarily to facilitate the production and export of sugar to England. So dominant were the plantations in the economic and political life of the island that right through the 1940s, despite rapidly declining sugar fortunes, they remained the largest source of employment.

As if to prove that nothing had changed, in the century following emancipation, St. Lucia fell into general decline and depression. Except during World War I, sugar prices declined uninterruptedly, sugar factories closed down, and since the fate of the economy was tied to sugar as sugar fell so did the economy.

Many black farmers who after emancipation had so

zealously taken to the land soon had to face the harsh reality that their holdings were either too small or too inaccessible for the cultivation of the export or cash crops, and the local market for the ground provisions and other food crops that they produced was limited and sometimes unreliable. To satisfy their basic material needs they had little choice but to offer their labor to the plantations, if not full-time, at least part-time.

Yet with dwindling profits, a failing economy and, more importantly, an influx of indentured labor, plantations were under no pressure to improve the wages and working arrangements of their laborers. Instead planters demanded prolonged work days at stagnated wages, and workers continued to live in houses no different from the sugarcane and coconut thatched huts with mud flooring that they had occupied during slavery. As late as the 1930s when a shilling could buy only two pounds of fresh meat, or three pounds of fresh fish, or six pounds of rice or flour, daily wages for laborers ranged from one shilling to one shilling and six pence for men, and ten pence to one shilling for women.

During this century of deprivation there were intermittent periods of economic relief, but they all proved transitory. The first of these reprieves from the country's economic woes came in 1886 when Castries became a refueling station for coal-burning steamers. Ships brought in coal that was piled on the pier into black mountains that dwarfed not only the waterfront but the coal-bearing ships themselves. The coal was then reloaded onto coal steamers calling in for refueling. All the unloading and reloading of the coal was done by manual labor.

Using shovels, barebacked men covered with coal dust and sweat filled hundred weight bamboo-thatched baskets with coal, and with the women holding on to one end of the baskets and the men the other, the hundred weight baskets were loaded onto the women's heads. Then, with backs straight as electric posts, necks taut as pulleys, heads wrapped with mandra cloth, waists wound tight with rope or cloth, and with nothing between their heads and the baskets of coal but small pads resembling miniature pillows, the women, faces shining with sweat and coal dust, and like goddesses carrying oversized umbrellas, joined the procession of similarly loaded women that stretched like a marathon from the mountain of coal and up ladders leading to the ship. After climbing the ladders the procession of women entered the ships, descended into storage rooms and deposited their loads, coal dust rising to their faces. And when ships came for unloading, the women unburdened them in the same manner as they did the reloading, only this time instead of unmaking the mountain of coals, they rebuilt them. And when like a pyramid the mountains rose above their heads, they climbed steep ladders to dump their hundred weight cargoes on top of the heap, as if to outdo the pyramids their distant ancestors constructed millenniums ago.

These coal refueling activities and the reconstruction that went into remodeling the harbor into a coal-fuel station provided employment for many St. Lucians whose land holdings were too small to be fully self supporting, or who couldn't find adequate employment on the plantations. But by the 1920's, coal was giving way to oil as a source of fuel so employment in the coal refueling business took a down turn. For example, coals loaded unto coal using steamers at the Castries coaling station declined from 27,400 tons in 1919 to 5501 tons in 1921.

In 1889 Castries became home to a naval garrisoned station, and before long detachments of the West India Regiment and the Royal Artillery were stationed there. The several years of construction activities that resulted, and the economic activity the presence of the military generated attracted workers not just from the villages and countryside of St. Lucia but also from neighboring islands like Barbados. But this too was short lived. The military pulled out sixteen years later in 1904, leaving such an economic void that one visitor felt compelled to comment that *"St. Lucians saw poverty staring them in the face, for they had lived like parasites upon British soldiers for so long that they had nothing left to fall back on."*

Another economic respite came with World War I when the troops returned, and sugar prices rose causing increased production and employment, and again during World War II when the Americans established a Naval base at the northern end of the island in Gros Islet, and an air base at Vieux Fort. The construction activities and employment that resulted created such an economic boom that, for example, Vieux Fort was transformed from a small fishing and sugarcane village into a town with a severe housing shortage. Its cane fields were turned into a network of runways and horse-shoe shaped earth-mounds, inside of which were bush and paved strips of roads extending to the network of run- ways. The earth-mounds served as   camouflaged hangars for war planes. To make way for the main run- way (Beane Field Airport), the course of the Vieux Fort River was altered to flow more westerly. In addition, the Americans built roads, port facilities, sewage systems, water reservoirs, bridges, a fire station, and a hospital where injured soldiers could layover en route from Europe to America.

Even so, the coming of the Americans created lasting social and economic problems. Their easy money spoiled many young women into prostitution and inculcated a legacy of dependency. So although Vieux Fort has become a commercial center for surrounding villages and hinterlands, the fishing and industrial capital of the island, and home to the island's only international air-port, and home also to one of two ports capable of accommodating ocean-going vessels,   up to the year 2002 the town's residential area was dominated by two ghettos, one on the east side and the other on the west. The one on the eastern side had sprawled over an area with disease infested open ditches, no running water, and where pigs once roamed. The surrounding bush and water front were still toilet to many.

The greater share of the employment that develop-ment brought to Vieux Fort had gone to people from other towns, villages, and farming communities. Vieux Fortians, they said, were lazy, tardy, unreliable, and dis-respectful of authority. Some say Vieux Fortians were sitting around waiting for an American second coming.

Historian, Dr. Jolien Harmsen, in her book, *Sugar, Slavery and Settlement: A social history of Vieux Fort, St. Lucia, from Amerindians to the present*, presented a dif-ferent view of Vieux Fort. Vieux Fort, she explains, has been a victim of its geography. Vieux Fort's large expanse of flat land made it ideally suited for sugarcane cultivation. This was great for the plantation owners but bad for the slaves. The absence of mountains made it near impossible for the slaves to run away to freedom, and since most of the plains of Vieux Fort were suitable for sugar cultivation, there was little of the so called marginal lands for the slaves to grow their own food. Therefore, more than most other parts of the island, the slaves in Vieux Fort were heavily dependent on the plantations (someone else) for their survival.

Even when slavery was abolished the dependency remained because there still wasn't any land (marginal or otherwise) to be had. After all, the plantations did survive slavery. When the Americans came and replaced the sugarcane fields with a military base (a direct result of Vieux Fort's geography), the dependency syndrome got even worse because not only did the military base occupy the whole of Vieux Fort but it provided unprecedented high levels of employment and wages. More recently Vieux Fort's expanse of flat lands has made it the beneficiary of other windfalls, among them an international airport, a government livestock farm (the largest on the island), a national stadium, and the largest industrial park on the island.

So unlike the striking farmers of 1993, Vieux Fortians, according to Dr. Harmsen, have learnt that they are not deciders of their own fate. Slavery, sugar, the Americans, Halcyon Days Hotel, the Winera Paper and Paperboard Mill, the Heineken Brewery and the container transhipment center are some of the things and events that to them have been the decider of their fate. Accordingly, many Vieux Fortians sit and wait for the next opportunity, the next decider of their fate, that they hope to quickly exploit and then wait again for the next decider.

So Dr. Harmsen may be right. It is not that Vieux Fortians are lazy, but rather that they have learnt their history well, probably too well for their own good.

In spite of the intermittent economic reprieves that coal refueling and British and American military activities brought, the economic plight of laborers was such that between 1901 and 1911, some 8,217 or 16 percent of the population migrated, some to work on the Panama Canal, some others in the gold mines of French Guiana. During that decade the country's population declined by 2.5 percent, from 49,883 to 48,637.

Responding to their economic plight and worsening work conditions, laborers often struck back at their employers. In 1849, just ten years after emancipation, workers were lulled into the false sense that they were in control of their fate. They revolted, burning several estates. The government invoked the mutiny act and had eight of their leaders shot. History repeated itself in 1907. The coal-carriers in Castries went on strike, and while waiting to secure a hearing from the governor, they destroyed provision shops and looted the Castries market. The strike soon spread to the Cul-de-Sac sugar factory. There, a company of twenty-two policemen, upon clashing with the strikers, fired into the crowd, killing four and wounding twenty-three. A few days later the arrival of the warship H.M.S. Indefatigable at the Castries wharf helped quell the strike. Clearly, based on the outcome of both labor uprisings, the sympathies of the white-planter dominated government did not lie with the workers. And history repeated itself yet again when, eighty-six years later, October 1993, striking farmers protesting against low banana prices and an allegedly corrupt SLBGA, pelted police with bottles and stones. The police responded with gun fire and the result was two deaths in the valley.

During this century of economic ill, even nature seemed to conspire against the people. In 1854, just sixteen years after slavery, a cholera epidemic struck, claiming (by one account) about 1,500 lives out of a population of 25,000. So quickly did the victims fall that the island had to resort to mass graves. As a legacy of slavery marriages weren't very common among the recently freed, but with the plague many couples rushed to the altar. Marriages during the months of the epidemic increased four to six-fold over the previous year. Indeed, the number of children born within wedlock doubled from one out of four in 1853 to one out of two in 1962. For several generations the epidemic would live in the psyche of the nation as *En temps Choléra*.

Then came the great landslide of 1938, when after heavy rains the hillsides overlooking the Cul-de-Sac

River, along the villages of L'Abbaye and Ravine Poison, burst open releasing mountains of mud and rocks. On its way to the river the avalanche swept away and buried everything in its path, leaving in its wake tons of debris, mud, boulders, flattened houses, uprooted trees, and human and animal body parts. When the dead and missing were counted, the people of L'Abbaye and Ravine Poisson found out they had ninety-two friends and relatives to mourn for, ninety-two friends and relatives for whom to hold all night wakes of coffee, rum, katumba, and stories of past disasters, few to match the great landslide of 1938.

Ten years later, in 1948, as if to outdo the deeds of the landslide, came the great Castries fire that incinerated three-quarters of the city into a wilderness of ashes, smoldering coals, burnt galvanized sheets and concrete foundations. When the ashes settled, 809 families or 2,293 people were homeless, nine million dollars of property was lost, and many irreplaceable documents were destroyed, prompting the then eighteen-year-old Derek Walcott to immortalize the event in his famous poem, *A City's Death by Fire.* All this when just twenty-one years earlier, in 1927, another fire had consumed seventeen blocks of the city, including most of the business district. Nevertheless, one good thing came out of the 1948 fire. The hectic construction that followed caused a well-needed boost in employment and economic activity.

What all this history would have made clear to the 1993 striking banana farmers was that be it the early demise of the Caribs, the establishment of sugar as the dominant crop in the 18th century, the importation of Africans for slave labor, the subsequent abolition of slavery in the 19th century, the importation of indentured labor as a substitute for slave labor, the transformation of Castries into a coal refueling station, or the establishment of military bases in the 20th century, most of the inhabitants of the island never had a say in any of the major events that have determined the very nature and composition of their island. But refusing to take a page from some of their fellow citizens of Vieux Fort who had long bowed to the vicissitudes of history, farmers went on a strike and history repeated itself.

10

The Valley Of Death

O bviously, farmers had not consulted with historians, and even if they had it was very unlikely that they would have paid them any mind. After all, they hadn't heeded the many voices of reason that rang across the nation. Besides, rarely does passion go to bed with reason. So what seemed destined to happen, happened on the afternoon of the third day of the strike, an October afternoon that though in the middle of the hurricane season showed no signs of rain, nor was there much of any wind. Instead, the valley was bathed in a sunlight that reflected off the banana fields, accentuating their bluish-green vigor.

Strewn across the highway that snaked through the valley, parting the banana fields into halves, were felled coconut and mango trees, burning tires, junked vehicles—even a forty-foot container—and whatever other instruments of barricade farmers and their supporters could find. Farmers had suddenly turned engineers, proving that bananas were not the only things they could produce.

Alongside the highway and fronting the homes, gas stations, and stores that have broken the monopoly bananas had on the valley, were crowds of farmers, their supporters, and others seizing an opportunity for excitement, entertainment, and lawlessness. Beyond the strip of encroachment, beyond the crowds of protesters (armed with stones, bottles, and pent up anger), the banana fields stretched to the bottom of the verdant hills rimming the valley. To the right, beyond the banana fields, the hills rose to form the villages of Richfond, Derniere Riviere, and Au Leon.

Armed with a tractor, machine guns, shields, and a direct order to take whatever steps necessary to restore law and order, the police advanced along the highway intent on undoing the work of the farmers and their supporters.

Not to be out done, protesters pelted the police with

rocks and bottles. They were unafraid because there was no precedent in living memory of police firing into a crowd. Besides, if the police did fire, they were pretty sure that it would be teargas or blank shots and not live bullets that would come their way. Things that could hurt but not kill. By then some farmers had reached the point where they were willing to endure anything short of death to carry their message across the length and breadth of the nation. On Wednesday, the first day of the strike, under a barrage of stones the Prime Minister, himself a banana farmer, had in the manner of Shadrach, Meshach, and Abednego driven through a barricade of burning tires. Drove through as if the barricading infernos was nothing more than a banana leaf across the road. The pelted rocks simply bounced off his car, and after he got through the barricade his car showed not one sign that it had just gone through a furnace. But to the great thrill of the protesting farmers and their supporters, the next person who attempted the feat of the Prime Minister wasn't so lucky. His car caught afire and burned to uselessness.

Emboldened by these happenings, short of death, farmers were ready for the police. But they had made a miscalculation. The police were not made of steel. Besides, unlike the previous two days of the strike, they were now armed with the command that they should restore law and order at any cost.

A stone thrown by a farmer cracked through the shield of one policeman causing serious injury. One down. The police opened fire in the direction of the pelted objects, smoke from their guns mingling with that of the burning tires, gunshots ringing across the valley and carrying the story over the bananas to the villages on the hilltops, the acrid smell of bullets mixing with the odor of the perspiring crowd of police, protestors and spectators.

The protest turned into fear, panic, confusion and chaos. Suddenly, it was everyone for himself. Suddenly, the group objective of disallowing passage across the valley (hence the barricades) turned into each person seeking to preserve his own life. In the aftermath, after the smoke, confusion, sound and smell had died down, two farmers lay dead, several others injured, and two policemen admitted to the hospital, one of whom requiring nine stitches.

The nation was shocked and mesmerized. Suddenly what St. Lucians never imagined could happen on their soil, what they had reserved for troubled countries like Bosnia, Israel, and Ireland did happen. The notion that St. Lucia was a peaceful country, a place where people looked out for each other, was shattered, probably for good. Over-night the country, it seemed, had lost its balance, had lost its innocence. Dumbfounded, the old people were no doubt yearning for yesteryear. The young constantly complaining that the island had nothing to do, no where to go, for once did not lack for excitement. Suddenly, their country had joined the league of big countries.

One could well imagine St. Lucians abroad, those who saw their country as a safe haven, a place to which they could always return when they had had enough of the stress, crime, discrimination, and second class citizenship of their adopted countries, now fearing that their homeland could no longer provide them sanctuary. Hotel owners, the St. Lucia Tourist Board, the St. Lucia Hotel and Tourism Association, the Southern Taxi Association, the National Development Corporation, the Southern Tourism Development Corporation, and other stake-holders of the tourism industry were left to wonder how much the happenings in the valley had undermined their investments in tourism infrastructure and in their promotion of the island as a tourist destination. The St. Lucia Tourist Board was no doubt alarmed that its well thought out promotional slogan, *Simply Beautiful*, would no longer ring true.

Those concerns weren't misplaced. Soon after the shooting, St. Lucian overseas mission and tourism offices were flooded with inquiries about the safety of vacationing in St. Lucia. Airline ticket agencies received many travel cancellations. The US embassy in Barbados prepared contingency plans to evacuate its citizens.

11

Food of The Gods

To be fair, St. Lucian and other contemporary banana farmers were not the only ones to have paid homage to the banana. Originating in southern Asia in such lands as northeastern India, Burma, Cambodia, southern China, Sumatra, Java, Borneo, the Philippines and Formosa, the banana can proudly take its place along side corn, wheat and rice as one of the pillars of civilization, for its cultivation dates back to the dawn of civilization and as such it was one of the first foods of man. Indeed, some horticulturists believe that bananas were the earth's first fruit.

It is no wonder that in some ancient cultures the banana has occupied no less a position than that of a deity. In India, for example, the banana was called the F*ruit of the Wise Men* because according to an ancient legend the sages of India rested under its shade and refreshed themselves with its fruit. Another legend has it that the banana flourished in the Garden of Eden where its fruit was the source of knowledge of good and evil, hence it was also called the *Fruit of Paradise*. Not to be outdone, in the Koran the banana plant is referred to as the *Paradise Tree*, and in Buddhism the banana is sacred to one of the forms of the Goddess Kali and is worshiped on the third day of the month of Sravana.

The devotion of the ancients to bananas isn't without substance for few foods come as close to providing all of the nutrient needs of the body as does the banana. The fruit is considered one of the world's most important sources of carbohydrates. Pound for pound (edible portion) it yields more calories than any other fruit, and compared with the commonly used vegetables only corn and some legumes yield more calories than it. In fact, experiments suggest that bananas contain about 20 percent more calories than do potatoes.

The banana was found to possess significant amounts of all the essential minerals, including potassium, sodium, magnesium, calcium and iron. Furthermore, these minerals occur in such proportions that when the banana is eaten, an alkaline effect is produced that provides a corrective measure for the acidic tendencies of many common food stuffs, including bread, cereal, and meats. So much so that like oranges, apples, muskmelons and potatoes the banana is a good preventative and cure for acidosis.

Regarding vitamins, the banana was found to be a good source of vitamin A. At least as good a source as vegetables like green peas that are fairly rich in the vitamin. In vitamins B, the banana was also considered a good source and pound for pound was equivalent to the vitamin B contents of tomato juice and nearly equal to that of milk. Likewise, the banana has been found to be as rich a source of vitamins C as oranges and tomatoes. The fruit has also been found to be a decent source of vitamin E. In fact, only in vitamin D were bananas found to be deficient.

A 100 grams or 3.5 ounces of the edible portion of bananas have been found to provide 88 percent of the recommended daily allowance for calories, 1.5 percent for protein, 0.28 percent for fat, 22 percent for carbohydrates, 9 percent for vitamin A, 21 percent for thiamin or vitamin B1, 3.8 percent for Riboflavin or vitamin B2, 4.4 percent for niacin, 47 percent for vitamin C, 1.1 percent for calcium, 3.5 percent for phosphorus, 4.5 percent for iron, and 9 percent for potassium.

All told, among the major groups of nutrients only in proteins and fats was the banana found to have insufficient amounts to be considered a perfectly balanced ration. Nonetheless, experiments have shown that a combination of bananas and milk eaten in proper proportions can constitute a complete food.

Bananas' usefulness as a source of food goes beyond nutrients, however. Besides the fruit's great taste, in its ripened state, when the carbohydrate has been converted into a very simple form, the fruit is highly digestible, more so than both cereals and potatoes, and for that matter than most starchy foods. Such is the palatability and digestibility of the banana that it has become an important source of baby food and serves as a preventative and cure for constipation in babies and young children. In treatment of sicknesses like interstitial nephrites (inflammation of the kidney) where the protein intake of patients' needs to be restricted yet energy levels maintained, the inclusion of bananas in the diet has proven to be an important treatment. Also, in cases where patients are suffering from celiac (chronic intestinal indigestion) and thus are unable to properly consume carbohydrates and fats, as one of the few foods that such patients can tolerate, ripe bananas are indispensable. Arguably, when digestibility, palatability and nutrition are taken into account, few foods come as close to the perfect food as do bananas.

Nutrition, palatability, and digestibility aside, the banana has plenty more going for it. Not only has the plant been found to produce more food per acre than any other crop, but unlike many other fruits the banana is in season year round. Another advantage of the banana is that one need not worry about contamination. Its thick peel, which forms over 30 percent of the fruit, provides tight-proof protection against dirt, bacteria, and most other germs. And once away from the field the fruit is immune to insect pest. For example, worm eaten bananas are unknown. Yet, to top it all, the banana is a great buy. Even in temperate countries where the fruit isn't grown and has to be imported, the banana has been found to cost less (per food value) on a year-round basis than most fresh fruits and commonly used vegetables.

In terms of variety of use, the banana fares just as well. It can be cooked green and eaten as a vegetable, as for example, green figs and saltfish, St. Lucia's national dish. In its ripened state the banana can be unceremoniously eaten as a fruit. But if some ceremony be desired, the fruit can be sliced and eaten in milk, with or without cereals. It can serve in fruit salads or fruit cock-tails. It can be served in gelatine, custard, yogurt, or ice cream. It can be used to make cakes, pies, salads, chips, nectar, juice, jelly and jam. The banana pulp can be oven or sun-dried to produce a fig-like product.

Yet in some cultures, parts of Africa for example, where life revolves around the banana they take its usefulness even further. They use every inch of the plant. The dry leaves and dried peel of the trunk (pseudostem) are used as fibre to thatch huts, weave baskets, and to make rope. After a bunch is harvested, the pseudostem is chopped up and fed to animals. Regarding the fruit itself, besides its regular uses as fruit and vegetable the green banana is peeled, dried and grounded into flour and starch, and the ripened fruit is fermented into beer and wine.

Given its myriad uses, it is hard to imagine that the banana wasn't always the fleshy, delicious fruit that it is today. Back in the mist of time the banana had little or no pulp, instead, much like a pea pod, it consisted of an outer shell filled with large inedible seeds. Two competing theories explain how the banana emerged from inedible seeds to the seedless fleshy fruit worthy of St. Lucia's national dish, worthy of food for the gods. One theory employs hybridization (the intercrossing between species and varieties) to explain the appearance of the seedless banana. During hybridization, which is a natural occurrence, it is not unusual for a large number of new plant forms or varieties to simultaneously emerge. Thus, according to this theory, the seedless form of the banana suddenly appeared after such hybridizations. And realizing the food value of this hybrid, early man preserved it by propagation. In the other theory the development of the seedless banana wasn't as sudden, but rather followed a more dialectic process. According to this theory early man took care of the suckers of the banana plants that yielded the most flesh and the least seeds, so overtime through this process of selection, not unlike the evolution of species, a banana plant emerged with no seeds and all flesh.

However it evolved, the food of the gods has made its mark on earth. And with regard to St. Lucia, it is arguably the single most important post-slavery event that to date has help shaped the nation and its people.

12

Gone Bananas

The inhabitants of St. Lucia may not have had any say in the banana making a home on their island, nor in the shipping and marketing arrangements of the fruit, but once the industry was firmly established their fate was inextricably linked with that of bananas. What with a sugar industry in its death throes and an island beset by poverty and despondency, the people responded to bananas as if it were God-sent. And it seemed that indeed the banana was God-sent. Most of the population had access to only a few acres of land at the margins of the plantations or in the island's hilly interior, but with bananas this wasn't much of a problem because unlike sugar, bananas were well suited for small scale operations.

The crop's planting material, suckers they are called, is easy to transplant and transport. The plant is adaptable to a wide range of terrain, including hillsides, and being a year-round crop means that cash flow problems, a major constraint small farmers face, are minimized. The fruit allows intercropping so small farmers who then as now were the main producers of food crops need not totally sacrifice food crop production for banana production, the cash crop. In fact, since crops interplanted with bananas benefitted from the fertilizer and some of the other cultivation practices applied to banana plants, banana production sometimes complemented food crop production. Bananas have a shorter gestation period (less than a year) than most tree crops, so a banana field can be established quickly, a very important fact given the destruction that the island's hurricanes bring to the crop each year. Banana cultivation produces as a by-product a lot of vegetative trash that helps to replenish the soil and reduce the need of cash-strapped farmers for expensive fertilizers. Finally, given that farmers had access to a very limited amount of land, it was a plus that bananas yielded many times more food per acre than other staples like corn, potatoes or wheat.

Still, the SLBGA and the government did not leave anything to chance. The government built an extensive network of feeder roads that penetrated deep into the interior of the island, making lands accessible that once could only be reached by footpaths. The SLBGA established banana buying points along these feeder roads, eliminating the need for farmers to take their harvest all the way to port. They also gave farmers fertilizer and other inputs on credit, and established a crop protection insurance scheme that insured farmers' bananas against windstorm and hurricane damage. Meanwhile, WIN-BAN and the Ministry of Agriculture conducted extensive research on banana cultivation and sent a cadre of banana extension officers all over the countryside to educate farmers on the application of improved agronomic practices and the importance of keeping farm records.

For their part farmers had needed little encouragement to cultivate the fruit that was so compatible with their socioeconomic and resource constraints. With the crowing of roosters, men, women and children all over the island awoke from coconut fibre mattresses, picked up their axes, cutlasses, forks, and pickaxes, walked out of their straw and cow-dung thatched huts, and headed across rivers, uphill and downhill, deep into the interior of the island, to every nook and cranny, on top of steep slopes, on the flood plains of rivers and streams, on land infested by deadly snakes, anywhere that their feet could take them and where the soil was deep enough for banana plants to stand. There they waged war against virgin forests, against impregnable masses of vines, thickets, and trees. They felled and sawed the cedar, gomier and mahogany trees into lumber, and the branches and trees unsuited for that purpose they baked into coals. They set on fire the twigs, vines, under-brush, and branches that were too small to serve any useful purpose, and in the ashes of the fire they planted bananas, and between the banana plants they planted pumpkin, cucumber, legumes, and other crops that would bear fruit long before the planted bananas would spread out in full glory.

For many, before bananas, their only sure source of income was the once-a-year sugar cane harvest when they had to temporarily abandon their homes and travel across the island on foot to the sugar plantations and factories. Yet once their once-a-year sugarcane harvest income was spent they had little choice but to wait in misery until the next harvest. Worse, in many instances working in the sugar fields and in the sugar factories meant sexual abuse from overseers and plantation own-ers and losing one's spouse to them. Now, with bananas, they need not subject themselves to abuse, sexual and otherwise, and they didn't have to wait on anyone for wages.

The island took to bananas with such zeal that banana exports increased over a hundredfold from a mere 27 tons (worth EC$4000) in 1950, representing only 0.2 percent of exports, to 3.8 thousand tons (worth EC$490 thousand) in 1954, or 14 percent of all exports. Eleven years later, in 1965, the country exported 84.4 thousand tons, valued at EC$9.3 million and forming more than 83 percent of all exports. In fact, over the 1950-1965 period, banana exports grew by an annual average of 142 percent.

In sharp contrast, sugar exports, which had totaled 10.4 thousand tons in 1950, accounting for over 90 percent of exports, had by 1962 been reduced to zero and never again was the country to export sugar. A new era had begun. After two centuries of sugar domination bananas had finally replaced sugar as king.

One of the outstanding episodes of the dying days of the sugar industry was the 1957 sugar strike that took place in the very same valley where the 1993 banana strike had climaxed with the deaths of two farmers, marking what may well turn out to be the end of an era in the history of the banana industry in St. Lucia. By then sugar production and manufacturing had been reduced to the three great valleys—Cul-de-Sac, Roseau, and Mabouya. The Workers' Cooperative Union turned the

United Workers Union, having successfully leveraged itself into the St. Lucia Labor Party (the ruling Party), came up against the sugar factories. But facing decline, the factories were in no mood for negotiations. They refused to recognize the United Workers Union's right to represent sugar workers, don't talk of yielding to the union's demand of increased wages. In typical fashion the union launched a strike that started at Roseau, then spread first to Cul-de-Sac and then to Mabouya.

It was then that Mr. John Compton, union activist, elected representative of the Dennery and the Mabouya Valley area, and a recent graduate of London University, emerged on the national scene when he entered the factory's compound to further articulate the Union's demands and found himself staring at the end of a gun held by the owner of the factory (Mr. Compton had also drawn his own gun). This image, this symbol of Mr. Compton as the man who, like David facing Goliath, had singlehandedly faced the enemy of the people, the enemy that had enslaved their ancestors, and returned unscathed and victorious, would leave an indelible mark on the memory of the nation and would help propel Mr. Compton into a political career in which he would dominate the politics of the nation for three decades.

The factory owners, like the striking 1993 banana farmers, but unlike the people of Vieux Fort, weren't paying any attention to history. Instead they secured governmental support. The magistrate invoked the Riot Act. Police from Barbados and Grenada joined those of St. Lucia. A British warship came to port. Sugar workers were so readily arrested and jailed that according to Mr. George Charles (then Chief Minister and Labor Party and Union leader) the Union went broke bailing them out. In Castries, on their way to joining sugar workers from the Cul-de-Sac Valley, Mr. John Compton and Mr. George Charles narrowly escaped the thrusting bayonet of a policeman. On a different occasion, police guards fired at Mr. Charles as he was walking out of the Cul-de-Sac Sugar factory.

By the fifth week of the strike the Union concluded that if the strike didn't end soon it would turn into a civil war, so to hasten matters it spread the strike to banana workers and banana carriers in Castries, which effectively put a stranglehold on the country. A few days after, the factories came to the negotiating table. The rights of the union for collective representation was recognized. Workers got wage increases. The factories agreed to improve the methods of transporting canes by wagons to avoid spillage and to constantly inspect the scales used for weighing task-workers' harvested canes.

After the settlement, the same Mr. Compton, himself a banana farmer, who forty years later, in 1993, would admonish farmers against a strike and, when they did strike, after driving unscarred through a wall of fire had equipped the police with the statement that they should restore law and order at whatever cost necessary, and so armed the police had brought death to the valley, was brought to court and convicted and fined for disturbing the peace. Five years later (by 1962) all the sugar factories on the island were silent, serving as mere monuments that tourists marveled at and children on educational field trips visited to remind them of the cruelties of the past and that, notwithstanding the1993 striking banana farmers, there was something called history.

With sugar gone, giving bananas room to grow, the effect of the fruit on the island's economy couldn't have been more dramatic. In 1950 with a gross domestic product of EC$10 million or a per capita GDP of EC$147, St. Lucia was the poorest of the Windward Islands. Twelve years later the country's per capita GDP increased to EC$303, reflecting a more than doubling of GDP to EC$27 million. Another eight years later, the economy almost tripled to EC$67 million in 1970 or a more than doubling of per capita GDP to EC$669.

These economic gains were even more impressive when one considered that the previous century had come with little sustained economic growth and plenty of poverty and despondency. Suddenly, farmers' grass and cow dung thatched huts gave way to wooden houses with galvanized roofs; mud floorings gave way to linoleum covered wooden floors; flambeaus and kerosine lamps to electric lighting; and donkey and horse drawn carts to automobiles. Suddenly, banks multiplied, primary schools and health centers appeared in the most isolated of villages, diseases such as malaria, bilharzia, and typhoid fever that once plagued the nation became almost nonexistent, roads stretched over mountains, rivers and valleys, running water penetrated into the very heart of the hinterland.

Yet farmers were not the only ones to benefit from bananas. The industry provided employment for banana extension officers, Geest and SLBGA office workers, banana selectors and tally clerks at banana buying points, truck owners transporting bananas from buying points to the ports, dock workers packing the bananas under the banana sheds, women banana carriers moving the fruit from the sheds to Geest banana boats, men relaying these bananas from the women's heads to the bosoms of the boats.

The banana boat visited the island weekly to pick up bananas, so every week every man and woman, no matter how poor, with an acre or half an acre or quarter of an acre of land could have money flowing into their pockets or the spaces between their breasts from the sale of bananas, no matter how few. And since most small farmers were at the lowest income brackets, their propensity to spend out of each additional dollar of income was greater than that of the population as a whole. Thus farmers were the dream come true of shop-keepers, turning towns like Vieux Fort, Castries and Soufrière into flourishing commercial centers, and bringing work to a host of tailors, seamstresses, black smiths, fishermen, lawyers, doctors, teachers, and owners of passenger transports, cinemas, rum shops and dance halls.

Still, the contribution of bananas could not be measured in economic terms alone. Unlike sugar, which was dominated by large plantations, small and medium size farmers accounted for the larger portion of banana production. The demise of the sugar industry and the accompanying rise of bananas implied, therefore, a rise in the number of small and medium scale farmers and, as we have seen, a relative improvement in their economic and social welfare. This also translated into an improvement in the distribution of wealth both geographically (since banana cultivation was much wider spread than sugar) and population-wise (since bananas suited both large and small scale operations). Therefore, if it be true that the economic empowerment of the masses is a prerequisite for political democracy, then one can conclude that the banana industry helped brought about an environment more conducive to genuine political democracy.

For here was a people less than a century removed from slavery who, when they did get their freedom, faced a sugar plantocracy and a government that did their best to debar them from a life independent of sugar plantations. A people who formed the clear majority of the population, yet the resources of the country weren't there for their benefit, but for the benefit of the colonial power and its surrogates. Slavery was abolished, yes, but the people lived a life at the periphery of the plantations, at the periphery of what was happening to and in their country.

Then came bananas and suddenly the masses were in the thick of it all. They were decision makers, deciding on how, when, where, and how much to grow of the fruit that would in time define the very character of their country. The banana became more than the bread and butter of the island. The banana became its very heart and soul. In as much as sugar was synonymous with slavery, bananas could be associated with freedom. Banana cultivation empowered the people because unlike laboring on the sugar plantations farmers cultivating their few plots or acres of bananas had to become self-reliant, responsible and forward-looking economic agents. After all, their livelihood now depended directly on the success of their own farming operations.

Economic independence emboldened farmers' participation in the political process. Banana sheds, buying points and boxing plants became rural halls where farmers met, socialized, discussed the issues affecting the banana industry, the issues affecting the country; how the government was helping or impeding the growth of the banana industry, how well the government was running the country. These discussions helped cement farmers into a voting block. After all, they shared something in common—bananas, their livelihood. And since such a sizable percentage of the population was engaged either directly or indirectly in banana cultivation, politicians and the government had no choice but to pay attention to the needs and wants of banana farmers. As such, farmers were not only deciding about banana production, they were helping to shape the nation, or rather the birth of the nation.

The cultivation of bananas touched the very social fabric of the country. One could well imagine teenage farm boys measuring their manliness by how many banana bunches they could carry, men measuring their worth, and women appraising their menfolk, by how many acres of bananas they had under cultivation, how healthy their banana fields looked, how big were their harvests. Bananas improved farmers' social, economic, and political clout relative to the rest of the population, and thus changed how farmers related to each other and to the rest of the population. Suddenly, being a farmer was nothing to be ashamed of; on the contrary, rather than signaling that one was still a slave, banana farming signaled a distancing from slavery. Teachers, civil servants, business persons could proudly proclaim that they too were banana farmers.

Bananas changed the physical and aesthetic landscape of the country. Before long it seemed that the whole island was covered with bananas, so much so that it was hard to imagine there was a time in which banana fields didn't dominate the landscape. Banana-day was a beehive of activity; one got the impression that everyone on the island was involved with the harvest. On those days it seemed that every vehicle one met on the road either had a load of bananas heading to port or was returning to some buying point for another load. All over the countryside, farmers—men, women and children—with trays of one, two, three, four or sometimes five stems of bananas were taking their harvest, across rivers, uphill, downhill, uphill, to roadsides, to buying points. Boxing plants and buying points buzzed with activity. Banana straws littered not just the countryside that gave birth to them, but also the towns of Vieux Fort and Castries. So much so, one got the impression that banana cultivation was more about the production of straws than of bananas.

That was the 1950s and 1960s. In the 1970's, as if to

remind banana farmers that despite their success story they were far from being in control of their destiny, barely recovering from Hurricane Beulah, which had destroyed 75 percent of the 1967 banana crop, severe droughts (between 1970 and 1977) devastated the industry, and just when bananas were about to recover from the droughts, Hurricane David in 1979 followed by Hurricane Allen in 1980 brought further calamity. Such were the effects of these natural disasters that banana exports fell by more than half from its 1969 peak of 86 thousand tonnes to 32 thousand tonnes in 1975, and then fell further to less than 30 thousand tonnes in 1980, the lowest in more than twenty years.

The decline of the banana industry led to an out-pouring of aid. The European (LOME Convention) Export Stabilization Scheme (STABEX) provided funds to launch a banana revitalization program that involved extending the network of feeder roads to more remote parts of the island and increasing banana yields through greater application of fertilizer and pesticides. The Development Division of the British Government financed a five-year (1977-1982) banana development program, and when the program ran out they put in place a three-year (1983-1986) Banana Industry Support Scheme. The United States, through its USAID depart-ment, reportedly contributed to the Eastern Caribbean an annual average of US$52 million over the 1980-1989 period.

Thanks to these international donors and to rising banana grower prices resulting from an appreciating pound sterling and to improved fruit quality (following the shift from boxing plants to field packing), bananas took off again in the mid eighties. Spurred on by these events, farmers cultivated bananas more extensively and intensively than ever before. So that by 1990 banana exports surpassed 130 thousand tonnes for the first time in the island's history and then climbed to a peak of more than 135 thousand tonnes, which up to 2002 had remained unsurpassed.

Joined by growing tourism, construction and service sectors, this period of record-breaking banana exports was accompanied by considerable economic expansion. Real GDP more than doubled from EC$484 million in 1980 to EC$1022 million in 1992, corresponding to a 78 percent rise in real per capita GDP from EC$4193 to EC$7459. In fact, with a real economic growth rate (GDP) of over 7 percent during the 1983-1992 period, St. Lucia emerged not just as the wealthiest of the Windward Islands, but as the country with one of the most viable economies in the Caribbean.

The island attracted immigrants from the likes of Trinidad and Guyana. Castries became a commercial and shopping center not just for the rest of the country, but as well for neighboring islands. In increasing numbers St. Lucians went to New York and Miami for weekend shopping. So well was the economy performing that like prophets of old some contributors to the local newspapers felt compelled to warn citizens to beware of their profligacy because the good times may not last forever. Despite the prophetic voices, mansions mushroomed all over the country, shopping malls sprang up, and, thanks to affordable Japanese reconditioned vehicles, cars started running out of roads, the number of pickup trucks in banana farming districts multiplied. Television and telephone penetrated the deepest interior of the island, secondary and primary schools spread throughout the land, farming villages like Desruisseaux, Augier, Mon Repos, Piero, whose (not long before) only sources of lighting were kerosene lamps and flambeaux bottles, blossomed and prospered into communities where the shacks and huts gave way to houses that would make any man proud. Almost overnight Castries and Vieux Fort were transformed into sprawling suburbs.

Then 1993 came along, and as in the 1970's things changed for the worse. The European Community became a single market, casting doubt over the continuation of the preferential treatment that St. Lucian bananas enjoyed on the United Kingdom market. Seizing upon the confusion, Latin American bananas flooded the market causing prices to fall. The exchange rate value of the pound sterling chose no other time to take a dive. Falling banana prices in the United Kingdom, a depreciating sterling, and financial abuse by the SLBGA combined to produce a banana growers' price that was well below most farmers' cost of production. Farmers responded. Their production fell to 123 thousand tonnes, 9 percent less than the previous year, and, accusing the SLBGA of corruption, they demanded that the SLBGA board of directors be disbanded, and that they, the farmers, should receive a guaranteed minimum price of 30 cents per pound of bananas. The country didn't heed the farmers' demands, so farmers, unmindful of history, went on a strike that brought deaths to the valley, marking what some perceived as the beginning of the end of the banana industry in St. Lucia.

13

The Birth of A Nation

If farmers had paid attention to history, they would have known that it was only beginning in the late forties and early fifties, over a century since slavery, that the inhabitants of the island began having a voice in deciding their fate. Yet, even so, the attaining of that voice had been a struggle. As pointed out earlier, up to emancipation the island had a Crown Colony government in which an Administrator who reported to the Governor of the Windward Islands presided over an

Executive and a Legislative Council. Along with the Administrator the Executive Council included an Attorney General, a Protector of Slaves and a Colonial Secretary and Treasurer. The Legislative Council, on the other hand, included members of the Executive Council, a Chief Justice and five of the principal proprietors on the island.

In 1924 the Legislative Council was modified to comprise an Administrator, an Attorney General, a Treasurer, a Registrar of the Royal Court, a Chief Medical Officer, an Inspector of Schools, three nominated members and three elected members. In spite of these changes the masses were far from having a voice in their governance. Not only was the Executive Council, of which there were no elected members, the chief organ of government, but to participate in the Legislative Council's electoral process, either as a voter or a candidate, one had to be both literate and possess substantial income or property, criteria that placed the little politics that existed in the country beyond the reach of most of the populace. So, long after slavery, the island was still not seen as existing to serve the vast majority of its inhabitants. In fact, one could well imagine the inhabitants themselves having problems accepting that the island belonged to them. After all, having come from a system in which they had no hope of owning anything, the notion that the island now belonged to them would

Sir George FL Charles

need cultivation before taking root.

Help came in 1951 when just as bananas were starting to take root on the island Great Britain introduced
universal adult suffrage. So no longer would politics be
the domain of only the educated and the well to do. At
long last the voices of the people would be heard. It was

a moment for which, if not the masses, the grass roots leaders of the people had long fought and waited. In the 1930's and 1940's, all over the British West Indies workers had gone on strike and rioted against unlivable wages and deplorable working and living conditions. Sometimes even paying with their lives, as happened in St. Kitts in 1935 when a plantation owner fired into a crowd of sugar workers (who came demanding higher wages), killing several of them. It had taken the entire police force and marines landing from a British warship to quell the riot that ensued. In most of the islands these spontaneous labor uprisings led to the formation of labor unions.

St. Lucia organized labor protests began with the formation of the St. Lucia Workers Cooperative Union, which was launched in 1939 and registered in 1940. Working as a time keeper on the 1945 construction of the extension of Vigie Airport (the same airport that many years later would honor him by adopting his name and erecting a statue of him), and having witnessed time and again the futile efforts of unorganized workers to secure better wages and working conditions from the administrators of the project, Mr. George Charles had needed little encouragement to join the union. Though mild mannered and of slight built, his voice would soon come to symbolize and champion the people's will for self-determination. In Mr. Charles the people had found a voice of struggle.

By 1951 the union was ready to champion the cause of the people, to lead the fight for self-determination. In its decade of existence it had successfully negotiated with the sugar factories and Castries bakeries for pay raises and better working conditions. Following a brief strike the union had forced the Colonial Development Corporation (in charge of rebuilding Castries after the 1948 fire) to the negotiating table where it won fringe benefits and a 20 percent wage increase for workers. The 1948 and 1949 Castries Town Board elections had left the union (for the first time) in full control of the Board, the second most powerful political organ in the country. Once in control, George Charles had promptly moved the resolution to make the Choc Cemetery a common burial ground for all, thus doing away with the stigma of the paupers' section and starting the process of claiming the island for the majority of its people. In addition, the union-controlled Board instituted a new wage structure for its employees that included higher wages, vacation leave with pay, improved promotional opportunities, gratuity and pension allowances, and overtime pay.

Encouraged by its successes, in 1950 the St. Lucia Workers Cooperative Union, renamed the St. Lucia Workers Union, had established its political arm, the St. Lucia Labor Party (SLP). So by the time the 1951 general elections came around, the first elections under universal adult suffrage, led by Mr. George Charles the labor union turn political party was poised to take over the mantle of national leadership, to take the fight a step beyond the struggle for better wages and working conditions to the struggle for self-rule. In this historical election the St. Lucia Labor Party won five of eight seats. The People's Progressive Party, also formed in 1950 and perceived as a Party of the middle and upper middle classes, won two seats, while an independent won the remaining seat.

There were two other important changes in this post universal suffrage government that gave the people an even stronger voice than before. Elected members on the Legislative Council increased from three to eight, so for the first time the number of elected members surpassed the number of those who were nominated. And for the first time the Executive Council now included some elected members (three). To summarize, after the 1951 general elections the Legislative Council comprised the Administrator, the Government Treasurer, a Crown Attorney, three nominated members and eight elected members. The Executive Council included the Administrator, the Government Treasurer, the Crown Attorney, one nominated member and three elected members.

Although those changes had given the masses a

voice in government, there was still a long way to go before the reigns of government would finally fall into their hands. The changes so far had simply given the people a voice, but not much else. For example, though the SLP had a clear majority of elected members in government, the first SLP resolution introduced (by George Charles) in the Legislative Council, which sought to legalize holidays with pay, met with defeat. The island received further help in its quest for self-determination when on March 15, 1956 Britain introduced a ministerial system of government. By then bananas had long surpassed sugar as the island's main economic activity and was well on its way to setting off a socioeconomic revolution. The masses had already participated in two post universal suffrage general elections, and had already tasted the political empowerment and economic independence brought about by bananas. St. Lucians (including Mr. John Compton) were returning home from London as lawyers, doctors, economists, eager to join the fight for self-realization.

Having won two general elections, the St. Lucia Labor Party had consolidated itself into a formidable champion of the people. For self-rule, the politicians were ready, the people were ready, the country was ready.

Under the ministerial system, the Executive Council was still recognized as the policy making authority of the government, and as such it consisted of the

Administrator, three official members, four elected members, and one nominated member. In the September 1954 general elections the Labor Party had won five of the eight elected seats, so it wasn't surprising that all four of the elected members that the Legislative Council voted to the Executive Council were of the Labor Party. The ministers of government were to come from the Executive Council, thus the Labor Party became the first government that was of the people and by the people. This first labor Government included George Charles, Minister of Social Affairs; Dr. Karl G. LaCorbiniere, Minister of Trade and Production; Herman B. Collymore, Minister of Communication and Works; and Clive A.M. Compton, Minister without portfolio.

With the ministerial system the people had taken yet another step toward self-rule, but their hands were still tied. The responsibility for financial matters remained with the Governor of the Windward Islands through the Financial Secretary. And when government department heads disagreed with ministers they could lodge their complaint with the Governor for final ruling. In addition, legislation proposed by the Executive Council had to receive the endorsement of the Colonial Office in England before they could pass into law.

On January 1,1960 Britain granted the country a new Constitution. The office of the Governor of the Windward Islands was abolished, and the Administrator

Sir John GM Compton

became the Queen's representative. The constitution brought major changes to the Legislative Council. The Attorney General remained its only officiated member. The number of elected members was increased to ten, while the number of nominated members was reduced from three to two. A Speaker, elected outside or inside the legislature, replaced the Administrator as President. In the Executive Council the Constitution made provisions for a Chief Minister and three other ministers, bringing the total number of ministers with portfolios to four. Championing the cause of the people, as leader of the Labor Party, Mr. George Charles became the country's first Chief Minister, responsible for Finance, Inland Revenue and Medical and Public Relations.

Soon after those constitutional changes, April 1961, as was required by Great Britain, the government called general elections at which the Labor Party won nine out of ten seats. By then Mr. John Compton had joined the Labor Party and had won his seat. However, disappointed that George Charles and not himself was the one appointed Chief Minister, he along with two other elected members left the Labor government and formed the National Labor Movement Party. With that defection the SLP majority was reduced to two seats.

A year later, responding to corruption and financial abuse in the St. Lucia Banana Growers' Association (SLBGA), Mr. George Charles followed the recommendations of the Biggs Commission (charged with examining the structure of the Banana Association) and proposed and passed legislation that transformed the SLBGA into a statutory body and barred members of the House of Assembly and the executives of political parties from serving on its Board.

On April 1, 1964, Messrs. J.M.D. and Allan Bousquet, both SLP elected members of the house, resigned from the Labor Party, citing dissatisfaction over the government's restructuring of the SLBGA as the reason for their departure. The Labor Party no longer had a majority in the house, so the Chief Minister, Mr. George Charles, had few options but to call a premature general elections.

To contest the elections held June 25, 1964, the People's Progressive Party joined forces with the John Compton led National Labor Movement Party to form the United Workers Party. Notwithstanding the new alliance, at that election the SLP faced an uphill battle. In 1961 Mr. Van Geest had gained ownership of the Roseau and Cul de Sac Valleys and factories, then the only sugar factories still operating on the island. In spite of Mr. Geest's promise at the time of purchase that the company would continue cultivating and manufacturing sugar in the Roseau Valley, by the end of the 1962 sugar crop year the company had closed both factories and before long bananas had fully replaced sugar in the valleys. That ended the commercial production of sugar in St. Lucia and many blamed the Chief Minister and the Labor Party for sugar's final demise.

The Labor Party had taken another blow when, with the restructuring of the banana industry, it fell out of grace with many farmers. Also, in Mr. John Compton it had found a formidable foe. He had emerged out of the 1957 sugar strikes in the valley as a champion of the people and as a political force that could not be ignored. With the Labor Party facing such odds, the results of the elections weren't surprising. The UWP, joined by two independents, won eight of the ten electoral seats, and Mr. John Compton, the chosen leader of his Party, became Chief Minister of government.

Three years after the 1964 general elections, March 1, 1967, St. Lucia attained Associated Statehood. The country took full control of its internal affairs, while Britain, in consultation with the government of St. Lucia, remained responsible for its defence and foreign affairs. Under Statehood the Legislative and Executive Councils were replaced by a Cabinet and a House of Assembly, and a local Governorship replaced the post of the Administrator as the Queen's representative. The first Governor under this new Constitution was Dr. (later Sir) Frederick J. Clarke. The Cabinet, to be headed by a Premier instead of a Chief Minister, would comprise five ministers, the Attorney General and the Secretary to the Cabinet. The House of Assembly would include the Speaker, ten elected members, three nominated members, and the Attorney General. As the leader of his Party, Mr. Compton made history when he became the first (and what would be the only) Premier of St. Lucia.

General elections came again in 1969, and with bananas still thriving and the Labor Party in disarray, the John Compton led UWP remained in power by winning

Sir Allan FL Louisy

six out of ten electoral seats.

With this defeat Mr. George Charles quietly bowed out of politics, but not out of history. Years later he was bestowed no less an honor than the Knighthood, Vigie, the nation's busiest airport was renamed after him, and in 2002 he was further immortalized when his statue was erected at the airport that bears his name.

Notwithstanding George Charles's retirement, the 1974 elections presented a different scenario from the previous one. For the first time since UWP got into power the Labor Party would become a serious challenge. Plagued by droughts, the banana industry was in sharp decline, but more importantly the Labor Party had gained an infusion of fresh personnel. Mr. Allan Louisy who had recently given up his judgeship at the Supreme Court of the West Indies Associated States to join the political foray had brought a boost of respectability and integrity to the Party. Moreover, the Labor Party was also profiting from a new crop of young, energetic, charismatic and college-educated members who had brought new ideas, great vigor and political and campaigning savvy to the party. In the 1974 elections the UWP had just managed to retain power by two seats, one of which was controversial.

On February 22, 1979, amid heated opposition from the Labor Party, St. Lucia attained its full independence from Britain. At long last the people were in full control, or so they thought, of their destiny. With independence St. Lucia's Parliament would include the Governor General, the House of Assembly and the Senate. The House of Assembly would comprise a Speaker, who may be elected outside the House, and seventeen elected members (seven new constituencies were added in 1974, bringing the number of elected members to seventeen). The Senate would comprise eleven Senators, six of whom would be appointed by the Governor

General on the advice of the Prime Minister, three upon the advice of the leader of the opposition Party and two in consultation with the general community. The first Governor General under independence was Sir Allan Lewis. The Cabinet, which remained the decision making body of government, would include the ministers of government led by a Prime Minister who replaced the Premier as the Chief Executive of government. As leader of his Party, Mr. John Compton made history again when in addition to being the first and only Premier of St. Lucia he became the country's first Prime Minister.

Besides independence, 1979 was an election year and the Labor Party carried with it great promise, excitement and fear.

Promise, because never before had St. Lucia assembled so many capable and educated candidates on one platform as the Labor Party of 1979. Just about everyone on the ticket held a college degree. There were lawyers, judges, agriculturists, educators.

Excitement, because the Party brought hope of defeating history, of making a clean break from the past. For the most part the George Charles led labor union turned political Party had been a voice of protest and a struggle for the rights of the working class. Under Mr. Compton, aided by bananas, the country had made great socio-economic strides, but the government had operated more or less within the structure laid down by

Britain. However, equipped with independence, the 1979 Labor Party promised to radically break away from the country's colonial and slave legacy and instead to begin the work of fostering black pride, national identity and self-realization. There was hope of righting the psychological damage of self-loathing and inferiority that slavery and then colonialism had heaped on the people. It seemed that for the first time since the ancestors of St. Lucians left the shores of Africa and India there was hope of total freedom—physical, mental and spiritual.

Fear, because having been out of power for fifteen years, it appeared that the Labor Party was willing to get in power by any means necessary. Just four years before it had been denied power by the thinnest of margins. The votes on the night of the 1974 elections had the UWP winning the elections by just one seat, but next morning a thorough counting of the votes had pronounced UWP the victor by two seats, an event so aptly captured by the title (*It'll be Alright in the Morning*) of a book by Rick Wayne, arguably St. Lucia's most preeminent and controversial journalist. This time around it seemed that the Party would let nothing come between it and power. At political meetings one candidate could be heard saying that if we can't get in power by the ballot then we shall get in power by violence. Moreover, rumors abounded that the Party had sent people to Cuba to train in the art of overthrowing governments,

George W Odlum

and the Party had received large caches of arms from Cuba's Fidel Castro and money from Libya's Muammar al-Qaddafi.

Fear also because it seemed that the Labor Party's promise of a clean break from the past was simply an exchange of one legacy for another. For example, the Party talked about land redistribution, taking from the "haves" to give to the "have-nots." It talked about nationalizing industries. It showed great disdain for tourism. The Party hinted that a multi party system was inappropriate for such a tiny country as St. Lucia, and it was clear that left to some candidates St. Lucia would have just one Party, and that Party would be the St. Lucia Labor Party. In brief, the perception was that the Labor Party would trade democracy for communism.

In the months leading to the 1979 general elections there were many signs that foretold the fall of the UWP government. Banana production had remained stagnant. Teachers were on strike for retroactive pay and higher wages. With Mr. Allan Louisy, the ex-judge, in its leadership ranks the Party had gained great credibility and prestige, and inspired by Mr. George Odlum the young crop of charismatic, college educated Labor Party candidates had become increasingly militant. Moreover, against the backdrop of a Labor Party promising to take from the "haves" to give to the "have-nots" many accused the UWP of losing touch with the people, of not caring about the plight of the masses, of being a bourgeois Party, a Party of the rich.

Two months before elections the youth of the island had begun to give a foretaste of what might come to pass should the Labor Party lose the elections. At UWP rallies they booed speakers. During the last few days of the campaign, as tension reached new heights, they took to pelting garbage at speakers. It got so bad that in some districts it was almost impossible for the UWP to hold public meetings. Two days before the elections, as the Prime Minister's car made its way down the streets of Vieux Fort, youths thronged the car, hitting it with sticks, and before the Prime Minister could roll up his car window a few protestors stuck in their hands and slapped him. Rarely had elections in St. Lucia sunk to that level of lawlessness and fervor.

So it was of no surprise, yet of great relief to many when just five months after being crowned the first Prime Minister of St. Lucia, Mr. John Compton and his United Workers Party were dethroned, ending a fifteen-year rule. The results of the 1979 general elections passed the mantle of leadership to the Labor Party by a twelve to five seat majority.

The days following the elections had been days of euphoria. The Party was so full of potential that expectations ran high. As a symbol of change and a break from the colonial past, the new government quickly changed the names of streets and recreational parks from their European-given names to the names of St. Lucian heroes. The new government was vibrant and energetic. In Castries, government ministers could be seen walking briskly between government buildings with a heightened sense of duty. In the midst of the euphoria, one St. Lucian minister of government addressing a function of the new revolutionary government of Grenada was alleged to have said that his only regret was that they (the Labor Party) hadn't come to power by a coup d'etat, then the revolution in St. Lucia would have been total. Shortly after the new government came into power, young men, many of whom were Rastafarians and were among those who allegedly had received arms to overthrow the government had the UWP won the elections, went on an island-wide rampage of rape and armed robbery. They were apparently too keyed up for a coup d'etat that wasn't forthcoming.

Six months after the elections a power struggle developed in the Labor Party government. The Party split into one faction led by Mr. Allan Louisy, and the other led by Mr. George Odlum. The Louisy faction controlled the Party machinery and was considered conservative and middle of the road. The Odlum faction was seen as espousing a radical and left of center political and economic philosophy. Even in appearance there was sharp contrast between the two men. In his forties, Mr. Odlum was heavily built and had an animated face and a voice that, though waxed eloquent, had still managed to hold on to some of its natural harshness. On the other hand, in his early sixties, Mr. Louisy was quiet, soft spoken and frail-looking. During the campaign many saw Mr. Odlum as the rightful and legitimate heir to the Party's leadership. For not only was Mr. Odlum one of the most visible and vocal campaigners of the Party but as an Oxford graduate who had held several senior national and regional administrative and policy-making positions, he displayed great intellect, spellbinding oratory and literary skills, and a genuine concern for the poor and downtrodden. In the eyes of many he was the rightful heir to the legacy of Mr. George Charles.

However, realizing that as Party leader Mr. Odlum's

militancy and combative rhetoric might drive voters away, the Party nominated Mr. Louisy as Party leader with the understanding that if the Party were to win the elections, after six months in office Mr. Louisy would relinquish the post of Prime Minister in exchange for the Governorship, thus making way for Mr. Odlum to become Prime Minister.

Six months expired, but citing that he didn't like the leftist direction in which Mr. Odlum would take the country, Mr. Louisy refused to resign as Prime Minister, thus inducing a power struggle in government. As the power struggle raged on, the Labor Party became increasingly demoralized. The Odlum faction accused the Prime Minister of incompetence and indecisiveness. They complained of blatant ministerial corruption and Mr. Louisy's appointment of what they considered inept ministers. Stating that the infighting in the Party was undermining his ability to function, Mr. Kenny Anthony resigned from his post as Minister of Education and sought the sanctuary of the university.

It seemed that even nature was against the St. Lucia Labor Party, against this experiment of thwarting the will of history. A few months after the 1979 elections, Hurricane David struck, destroying 70 percent of the island's banana crop. And not to be out-done, the following year Hurricane Allen struck, reducing the banana crop to nought and leaving the island's infrastructure in shambles. All that when bananas were still recovering from the droughts of the 1970's.

Nonetheless, like the striking 1993 banana farmers, unmindful of nature or history, the power struggle went full steam ahead. Less than two years after the Labor Party formed the government, In protest, the Odlum faction along with the UWP opposition voted down Prime Minister Louisy's 1981 budget. Taking that as a vote of no confidence in his leadership, Mr. Louisy resigned and the Governor General, in consultation with the House of Assembly, appointed Mr. Winston Cenac as the new Prime Minister of St. Lucia. The Odlum faction resigned from Cabinet and formed a new political Party, the St. Lucia Progressive Labor Party (PLP).

Soon, the PLP joined voices with the UWP in demanding an immediate dissolution of Parliament and the calling of fresh general elections. Before long, public support for fresh elections came pouring in. The Teachers' Union and the Civil Service Association went on strike. Cable and Wireless imposed a work stoppage. The island's ports closed down. The Chamber of Commerce ordered a total shutdown of stores and businesses. The country had come to a standstill. So bowing to the will of the people and the opposition parties, on January 15, 1982, the Prime Minister, Mr. Winston Cenac, announced that the government had been dissolved, that general elections would be held by July 1,

1982, and that a new government of national unity would preside over the country. The interim government, which would comprise five elected SLP members, and two elected members from each of the remaining parties, would have Mr. Michael Pilgrim of the PLP as its Prime Minister.

As Mr. Winston Cenac had promised, general elections were held on May 3, 1982. The UWP won fourteen seats, SLP two, and PLP one. So after fifteen years in power, followed by a less than three-year absence, the UWP Party with Mr. John Compton at its helm returned to power, bringing to an end even before it had begun the people's experiment in defeating history and becoming truly independent.

For his part, Mr. Rick Wayne once again came to the aid of the nation when he gave perspective to Labor's bungling of the government in his 1986 book, *Foolish Virgins.*

Coinciding with Mr. Compton's new reign, the banana industry rebounded, reaching unprecedented production and export levels, the country entered ten years of uninterrupted prosperity, turning it into the envy of the Caribbean and attracting high praise from such well respected publications as *The Economist.* Riding this wave of prosperity, Mr. Compton and his UWP went ahead and won general elections in 1987 and again in 1992. By then as one of the longest lasting and most successful political leaders in the Caribbean, Mr. Compton took his place alongside such Caribbean political stalwarts as Michael Manley of Jamaica, Eric Williams of Trinidad and Tobago and Grantley Adams of Barbados, in the process securing for himself no less an honor than the knighthood.

But just when Mr. Compton was probably beginning to feel infallible, probably thinking that the prosperity that his country was enjoying was due to his government and his government alone, and that his government and not what was happening on the outside was what was deciding the fate of St. Lucia, 1993 came along and history again made its presence felt. In response to the uncertainty surrounding the European Community's new banana policy, Latin American fruit flooded the market, banana prices fell, the pound sterling depreciated against the dollar, the price farmers received fell below their cost of production, farmers demanded a guaranteed minimum price of 30 cents per pound of bananas, the dissolution of the SLBGA Board, the appointment of a new Board, and the streamlining of SLBGA operations. No one paid much attention to the demands of the banana farmers. So going against history, farmers went on a strike that brought deaths to the valley and the subsequent fall of the United Workers Party after nearly three decades of political dominance.

14

The Evils of Bananas

Perhaps one reason the population hadn't been too responsive to the plight of farmers, even though bananas contributed such a large portion of the island's livelihood, was because at some level they had sensed that along with the good bananas came with plenty of bad. Not least among these was the indiscriminate clearing of the forest, especially on steep slopes, for the cultivation of bananas. Such degradation of the forest reached its zenith in the heady banana days of the mid-eighties and early nineties when most new lands available for banana cultivation lay on steep forested slopes, but encouraged by rising prices and infrastructural and financial support, farmers pursued the clearing of steep slopes at such alarming and unprecedented rates that there was a visible drop in the nation's water table. In those years not even the forest reserves set aside by government as water catchment areas were safe from land hungry banana farmers.

The thick canopy of the forest, along with its under cover of saplings, followed by a thick ground cover of dead leaves and branches, ensures that by the time rain water reaches the soil it has been reduced to a trickle, making it much easier for the soil to absorb the water. Moreover, the forest's well-developed root system, along with its host of soil microorganisms, help both the water retention and water infiltration properties of the soil. Thus, altogether, the forest's design allows the maximum amount of water to filter down into the water table which feeds the nation's rivers and springs. Even during an extended rain spell, when the soil has become saturated and the water then runs off, the deep root system of the forest helps to hold the soil and reduce erosion.

When the forest, especially on steep slopes, is replaced with bananas, the story changes drastically. As soon as rain water penetrates the single layer of banana foliage, it meets bare soil and a shallow root system that doesn't include taproots, and thus has limited ability to hold the soil. Accordingly, the amount of water that percolates through the soil and into the water table is reduced considerably. Instead, the water rushes into rivers and streams, carrying with it one of the nation's few natural resources—its delicate but fertile top soil. Some soil is deposited into the ocean where it is of no use but potentially can harm the island's fragile reef system. Some settle at the bottom floor of rivers as river sediments, and others clog the island's culverts and drainage systems. The lack of water infiltration and the high level of river sedimentation reduce the amount of rain it takes for the rivers to overflow their banks, causing frequent damage to agriculture and infrastructure. With the loss of top soil the land loses its fertility and its capacity to hold water. Thus, at each subsequent cycle of rain formation, there is less water to go around. As a result the country's water table has dropped considerably. For proof of that one need only take a look at the Troumassee River, once the largest river in St. Lucia, holding so much water that one could swim across, and which allowed boats to come inland. Now the flow has been reduced to a trickle.

Many farmers, however, see this as the nature of things, nothing to worry about. To some, if the island ends up with a water problem, it wouldn't be because of drying rivers but because of inadequate technology to draw the water from the rivers. It would be something to ponder that thanks to bananas a country once so blessed with water and rivers may one day have to import water or invest in expensive technology to desalinate sea water. If that becomes the case, St. Lucia's domestic and industrial needs may be satisfied, but what about water for agricultural use? Haiti, the first emancipated country in the Caribbean, the first country that had appeared to have defeated history, was once covered with forest—a tropical paradise. Now, with most of its forest gone, it has arguably become the poorest country in the western hemisphere.

Environmental pollution is another evil of the banana industry. So ironically the very same things—fertilizer, pesticides, weedicides, nematicides, fungicides—that helped the banana industry to achieve record levels of production in the eighties and nighties and made St.

Lucia the envy of the Caribbean, have undermined the nation's quality of life and long term viability. The chemicals applied to the soil are washed away into the rivers and hence the nation's drinking water. Some chemicals also leach into farmers' ground provision and vegetable plots, thereby making their way into the nation's food system. As ever more of the soil's nutrients are carried away into rivers, ever greater levels of fertilizer applications are needed to maintain yields. Moreover, the diothene tubes (some impregnated with the chemical, Dursban) that keep banana bunches blemish-free are littering and poisoning the countryside and the nation's rivers.

Cultivated primarily in a mono-crop culture, banana fields lack the biological control that would keep plant diseases and weeds in check, and maintain the nutrient replenishing capacities of multi-crop cultures. Thus, greater levels of chemical applications are required for optimal yields. On top of all that, there is the suspicion that the aerial spraying of banana fields for leaf spot is killing off the island's bird-life.

For years farmers have been handling dangerous chemicals without proper or protective clothing. One wonders to what extent banana chemicals have undermined the health of rural communities. After all, the toads have disappeared, so too have the fishes and the fer-de-lance. Bare-breasted women are still doing their laundry in the rivers as their mothers did before them, and their grandmothers before the mothers. However, besides adding their own pollution (detergents), one wonders whether it is still safe for them to be doing their laundry in the rivers. The country scene—women washing and socializing in rivers—now taken for granted, may need soon to disappear.

There is yet another evil: agriculture's over-dependence on one crop and St. Lucia's over-dependence on one economic activity. In the eighties and early nineties, farmers' over-dependence on a single crop became more so, for not only did they divert lands once devoted to food production into banana production, but to grow bananas more intensively many stopped the practice of interplanting food crops with bananas.

That tendency of farmers to produce bananas at the expense of food crops goes deeper than that, however. There are inherent structural biases that favor banana production to the neglect of other crops. A protected market, a well-defined and reliable shipping and marketing arrangement, institutional support that includes farm credit, research, extension services and the accessibility of inputs, combine to make banana production a much more attractive proposition than the cultivation of other crops. So much so that farmers would often choose the market certainty and production support associated with banana production over potentially more profitable crops.

The over-dependence of the country on bananas (or in general on any one single activity) puts it in a very vulnerable position. Any change (hurricanes, the depreciation of the sterling, increased competition) that negatively affects banana production and banana prices significantly undermines the nation's economy. Worse, the viability of the banana industry depends overwhelmingly on continued unilateral preferential access to the United Kingdom market. Thus the nation's livelihood depends to a great extent on whether or not another country feels like being generous toward it. The uncertainty that surrounded the new banana regime that the EC would adopt, which in part led to the 1993 banana strike, which led to a national crisis, provides an indication of the vulnerability of the nation.

As with sugar, right up to 1993, the country depended overwhelmingly on a single crop for its economic well-being, and the well-being of this industry depended on the fairness of a single shipping company, the reliability of a single market and the benevolence of a single (mother) country. So although with bananas the country had come a long way, as the 1993 striking banana farmers found out, albeit the hard way, it had come full circle. It seemed so much had changed, but nothing had

changed. The nation's fate was still being largely decided by what was happening beyond its shores.

15

Things Fall Apart

A fter the smoke, confusion, and chaos of the valley had settled, and farmers had returned to their homes, and the population was still pondering on how this could have happened and whether this meant the beginning of the end of the banana industry, the Prime Minister, himself a banana farmer, solemn and sorrowful, addressed the nation. The deaths in the valley, he said, was a "tragic climax" to three days of intense activity. He admitted that the SLBGA was in dire straits. It was bankrupt. In two years it had just about destroyed the banana industry. How did the SLBGA manage to do that? Through bad management and practices that came close to being criminal.

Its members traveled first class at the expense of farmers, such that their costs of attending conferences exceeded that of the entire government. Some directors were submitting claims for attending social functions and for each meeting held in a day. A 1990 fruit cutback program budgeted for $3 million ended costing $10 million. A pension scheme for farmers was voted down yet laid-off SLBGA employees were receiving tens of thousands of dollars in compensation. Worse, despite the dire situation of farmers, directors had voted themselves bonuses. Such were the dismal management and excesses of the directors that the association's finances had fallen from a EC$16 million surplus in 1990 to a debt of EC$23 million, EC$9 million of which was owed to Winera, the island's manufacturer of cardboard boxes.

From the Prime Minister's speech, not even farmers, the ultimate victims, were as innocent as they would like the nation to believe. Many, even after a mere sprinkle or the slightest of breezes, presented false claims to the Hurricane Insurance Fund. In 1992 alone, a year without any serious hurricanes, farmers submitted 7072 claims, costing the Association and therefore farmers as a whole

EC$2.3 million. One farmer was reported to have submitted thirty-five claims in one year, yet none of his neighbors had reported any damages.

The Prime Minister proclaimed that the Cabinet had agreed to dissolve the SLBGA Board of Directors with immediate effect, so "the way was now clear for government to act to preserve the industry and to ensure that it is operated in the manner that suits the best interest of the farmers. The government with the help of the Chamber of Commerce would begin the restructuring of the SLBGA." And with great resolve, the Prime Minister proclaimed that it is for the government to see "all areas of waste, extravagance, and fraud are eliminated, and the farmer gets his fair share which is not nibbled away by rats along the way."

But the Cabinet's decision to dissolve the board was largely redundant. Long before the announcement, in the face of the deaths in the valley, the SLBGA Board of Directors had completely collapsed.

Besides expressing sympathy with relatives of the dead and injured farmers, the leaders of the Banana Salvation Committee claimed victory upon witnessing the disintegration of the Board, and after listening to the Prime Minister, himself a banana farmer, admitting to the very grievances that they the farmers had lodged against the SLBGA.

Even so, the Prime Minister maintained that in view of the mob attack on the police with stones, bottles and cutlasses when all they were trying to do was to unblock the roads, "the action the police took, therefore, was one of self defense and completely justified."

Nonetheless the strike forced the Prime Minister to reflect on himself and history. After all, he too had been a victim, and he too was a banana farmer.

He said: "I have had my country house set on fire. I have had my banana sheds burnt and my property destroyed. I have cried to no one. I have picked up my broken tools and started over again. They may destroy my property but they will never break my spirit. I have seen this industry transform St. Lucia and its people. The grass huts and the ajupa on hills have given way to beautiful homes with water, electricity, television, and now telephone.

"I have faith in the banana industry and the people of St. Lucia. I seek no honor, no glory, no financial reward. My only reward is the advancement and progress of this country, which I have had the honor to lead for nearly twenty-five years and to serve for forty years.

"These are some of the things which sustained me on Wednesday (October 5, 1993) when I faced alone the angry mob at Richfond (part of the Mabouya Valley), an area which has benefitted so much from my work and personal sacrifice.

"About 36 years ago near the very spot, I looked down the barrel of the gun of the Barbadian police during the sugar strike. On Wednesday I looked into the faces of hatred, heard the curses from the very same throats of the people to whom but a few weeks ago I was Daddy Compton . . . so great was the hostile propaganda against me. But I remember the lessons of history and the Bible that the same voices which shouted Hallelujah will shout 'crucify him' without pausing for breath."

Clearly, unlike banana farmers, the Prime Minister, himself a banana farmer, was paying attention to history.

He went further to say that during the terrible moments at Richfond, where the boulders aimed at him and intended to kill came crushing down on his "humble pickup," he was shouted down as a "thief" and "murderer."

As to be expected the deaths in the valley brought plenty of blame. Besides the SLBGA's board of directors, the Prime Minister said that the blame for the deaths in the valley lay squarely on the people who had been quietly instigating, encouraging, and even financing the "criminal elements" and were now shedding crocodile tears. "They will carry the burden of guilt on their consciences—if they have consciences—throughout their lives. The deaths of these young men must continue to haunt them."

The opposition Party, the St. Lucia Labor Party, said plainly that the Prime Minister was squarely to blame for the deaths in the valley. The leader of the opposition said, "St. Lucian blood was shed and every drop must be accounted for." He called for the resignation of not just the Prime Minister, but as well that of the Minister of Home Affairs and the Minister of Agriculture. To prove how serious they were, the SLP threatened island-wide public meetings that would culminate in a mass rally in Castries where they would formally present a motion of "no confidence" in the government.

The police blamed the strikers. They said that for three days they had been bending over backwards to avoid violent confrontations with strikers. They said that it was only after a police officer went down from a striker's missile that pierced the officer's shield that they, the police, had been left with no choice but to return fire. Yet, when they did return fire, they did so only in the direction of the strikers' missiles. They said that the injured officer had needed no less than nine stitches to the head wound inflicted by the striker's missile.

The Deputy Commissioner of Police had this to add: "I have been around for a little over 30 years, and have seen violence in various forms in the life of this country. I have been outnumbered on several occasions by

Sir Vaughan A Lewis

crowds, very big crowds, but what I saw and what I experienced on this occasion defied belief."

The farmers, the Banana Salvation Committee, blamed first the Prime Minister for not heeding farmers' agonizing voices and for arming the police with: "take whatever actions necessary to restore law and order."

Secondly, they blamed the police, calling the deaths in the valley nothing less than police brutality.

Some SLBGA employees revealed that they themselves had been worried about the manner in which the affairs of the Association were being handled and they had repeatedly informed SLBGA management of those concerns, inferring, therefore, that management and the Board of Directors had no one to blame but themselves.

Not to be outdone, some ex-Directors of the SLBGA called the Prime Minister a liar. They said that while it was true that they inherited reserves of $16 million, it was also true that they inherited debts of $4.9 million to Winera, $4.2 million to input suppliers, and $500 thousand to the Windward Islands Crop Insurance. They further pointed out that during their term of office the Association had spent $10.73 millions to buffer farmers against falling prices and falling exchange rates. In fact, so blameless did the ex-Directors consider themselves that they threatened legal action of slander against the Prime Minister. One Director insinuated that the Prime Minister had no one else to blame but himself. He said that in the beginning Mr. Compton had ample opportunities to avert the strike, but he allowed it to happen so that in its aftermath he could restructure WINBAN to give the governments of the Windward Islands a 50 percent share instead of the 40 percent that farmers preferred.

The apportioning of blame notwithstanding, things soon changed. A farmer appointed Board of Directors replaced the pre-strike Board. The new board introduced measures to ensure farmers a minimum grower's price of thirty cents per pound of bananas. The European Union (EU) settled (in July 1993) on a new banana policy in which each of the African, Caribbean and Pacific banana exporting countries would be allowed to ship duty free a specified annual quantity (quota) of bananas to the EU, and shipments in excess of these quotas would be placed in the same category as bananas originating in South America and as such could be subjected to import duties and tariffs.

St. Lucia's annual quota was set at 127,000 tonnes. So, whereas prior to 1993 St. Lucia and the other Windward Islands could ship duty-free all the bananas the United Kingdom market could absorb, now no matter the size of the United Kingdom market, only 127,000 tonnes of St. Lucian bananas could enter the market duty-free. Clearly, the dismantling of the preferential treatment St. Lucian farmers had been enjoying was well on the way. In fact, the demand for the removal of banana trade restrictions was coming from no less powerful a country than the United States of America.

The cold war was over, the Berlin wall had already

come down, Castro was boxed in, the Soviet Union, once a great empire, was scrambling for financial aid, so the United States no longer had to worry about the islands in its "backyard" presenting a communist threat. So not only did USAID funds for the Caribbean dry up, but the American fruit companies had a US government actively campaigning for the dismantling of the preferential treatments that Windward Islands banana farmers were depending on for their survival. Another stack had been added to the problems of St. Lucian banana farmers.

More changes came. In 1994 the governments of the Windward Islands replaced WINBAN with the Windward Islands Banana Development and Exporting Company (WIBDECO), and two years later, WIBDECO and Fyffes Plc., each purchased a 50 percent stake in the buyout of Geest Bananas. WIBDECO's functions were to (1) negotiate marketing and freight arrangements for Windward Islands fruit, (2) manage the industry's investments, (3) reinforce the Windward Islands and Caribbean banana lobby in Europe, (4) arrange payments from export sales and other trading activities to the islands' Banana Growers' Associations (BGA's), (5) manage receiving and loading operations in the Windward Islands, (6) coordinate Geest shipping agency and branch operations in these islands, and (7) provide technical services to the industry to enhance productivity and fruit quality.

Still more changes. In September 1998, through the

Dr. Kenny D. Anthony

St. Lucia Banana Growers' Association (Dissolution) Act, the government dissolved the SLBGA, assumed all its $44 million debt, and vested its assets, liabilities, privileges and obligations in a new company, the St. Lucia Banana Corporation (SLBC) that would be privately owned by registered banana growers. The banana industry was now a completely private activity.

Soon the SLBC was joined by another company, the Tropical Quality Fruit Company (TQFC). Then in late 1999 the Agricultural Commodity Trading Company (ACTCO) joined the fray. So too did the Banana Salvation Marketing Company in the year 2000. The banana industry in St. Lucia then had four privately owned companies purchasing fruit from farmers and then selling their fruit to WIBDECO, who in turn sold to Geest of which WIBDECO itself owned a 50 percent share. Thus, if there were one thing farmers couldn't complain about, it would have to be choice of purchasing companies.

But in spite of all these changes bananas continued to fall. Production declined by 9 percent from 135 thousand tonnes in 1992 to 123 thousand tonnes in 1993, then again with the help of Storm Debbie it declined further by 26 percent to 91 thousand tonnes in 1994. The industry recovered briefly in 1995 and 1996, but then plummeted to a production low of 71 thousands tonnes in 1997.

Farmers were not the only ones to bear the wrath of a failing banana industry. In mid election term, in 1995, the Prime Minister, himself a banana farmer, decided it was time, after nearly three decades, to give up the mantle of leadership. But apparently unable to find anyone in his Party he deemed worthy of filling his shoes, of continuing his legacy, he selected Dr. Vaughan Lewis, previously Secretary General of the Organization of the Eastern Caribbean States (OECS), nephew of celebrated Nobel Laureate, Sir Arthur Lewis, and son of the distinguished Judge and ex Governor General, Sir Allan Lewis. To hand him the Prime Ministership, the Prime Minister requested of Mr. George Mallet, then UWP elected representative for Central Castries, to step down and allow Dr. Lewis to run for the seat in a bye-election. Dr. Lewis won the seat handsomely, and in a mid-election term St. Lucians awoke to find a New Prime Minister, an academician, not a banana farmer, or a lawyer, running the country.

Satisfied that his legacy would continue, Mr. Compton, no longer the Prime Minister, but still a banana farmer, took a back seat. But what he hadn't envisaged was that banana farmers, who may not care about history, had long memories and surely did care about politics. They remembered the words: "the police have been ordered to take all actions necessary to restore law and order." They remembered the ultimate price that their two brothers lying in their tombs had paid. So they simply bided their time until the next general elections.

And as if to make sure that farmers got their revenge, Mr. Kenny D. Anthony, whose name had since changed to Dr. Kenny D. Anthony, the Minister of Education under the failed 1979 SLP government who, in the middle of the SLP debacle had sought sanctuary at the University of the West Indies where he was serving as a law professor, returned just in time to lead the SLP, to lead the charge against the UWP. It was as if, not unlike Moses in the house of Pharaoh or Joseph in the land of Egypt, the university had been preserving Dr. Anthony all these years for the sole purpose of coming back to St. Lucia to take over the leadership of the country from where the Prime Minister, a banana farmer, had left off, and thus vindicate farmers for the deaths in the valley.

Even before the first words of the 1997 election campaign were shouted on the steps of the Castries market, the results of the election were a foregone conclusion because farmers remembered the words of the then Prime Minister that had brought deaths to the valley. The morning after the elections the news was out, the opposition Party had won sixteen to one. The farmers were jubilant. The ex-Prime Minister, himself a banana farmer, hadn't run for elections, but the farmers' victory was no less sweet. History had repeated itself. Bananas had again decided the fate of the island's political leadership. Bananas had helped to cause the downfall of Mr. George Charles, bananas had helped ushered Mr. John Compton into power, and bananas had brought his legacy to a close.

Nevertheless, in spite of the farmers' victory, bananas continued to decline such that by the year 2000 production had fallen to 70 thousand tonnes, nearly half its peak 1990 level, and banana export revenues had been reduced to EC$82 million or only 44 percent of the EC$187 million obtained in 1990. Accordingly, compared with the 7 percent real GDP annual growth rate the country enjoyed during the 1983-1992 period, over the 1993-2000 period real GDP grew by an annual average of only 1.7 percent.

Things got worse. In the closing months of 2000, Mr. Patrick Joseph, the Managing Director of the St. Lucia Banana Cooperation (by far the largest of the banana companies), a onetime official of the Banana Salvation Committee and a principal architect of the 1993 banana strike, whose vigorous campaign against the UWP during the 1997 election year was seen as instrumental in the SLP election sweep, was forced to resign his post amid a hail of accusations of corruption and misappropriation of funds, some of the very same accusations he had lodged against the SLBGA in 1993 that had led to the strike that had culminated in the deaths in the valley, and had brought to a close Sir John Compton's legacy. Yet, stout, bold, forceful and fierce talking, many a farmer had seen Mr. Joseph as the messiah who would restore the banana industry to its former glory.

Just like in the early eighties when bananas had been in trouble, European and government aid poured in. Government spent $600,000 relieving farmers (for five months) of the three cents levy they were required to pay for each pound of leaf spot (control) application, and at a cost of more than EC$1.4 million, it reduced by $1.00 (for four months) the price farmers paid for each carton. In addition, the government imposed price control on fertilizers and pesticides and exempted banana inputs and farm vehicles from all import duties and consumption taxes.

The European Community was reported to have contributed over EC$120 million for the recovery and restructuring of the banana industry. By 2001 the government had used $12.5 million of these monies to construct at Odsan, La Caye, and Vieux Fort banana inland reception and distribution centers. Another $22 million was used to fund variable farm inputs and to strengthen the banana (quality) certification program. In 2001 and beyond the government promised plenty more spending. Irrigation and drainage, agricultural diversification, land preparation and replanting, and the farm credit system were all candidates for additional funding. Yet, according to the government, the spending wouldn't stop there. There was something on the plate for even the farmers and their families who, because of poor land quality, could not compete and thus would need to leave the industry. They too could expect governmental help to ease their transition to a life without bananas.

Despite all that assistance, plagued by drought, leaf spot, and competition and strife among the banana companies, banana exports fell by more than 50 percent, from 70,281 tons in 2000 to 34,205 tons in 2001, the lowest in twenty years. Correspondingly, export revenues dropped by half to $43 million. Not surprisingly, real economic growth (real GDP) slowed from 3 percent in 1999 to under 1 percent in 2000 to -5.4 percent in 2001, causing some businesses to fold and others to restructure.

Accusing the government of playing a game of smoke and mirrors, Mr. Odlum, elected SLP representative and Minister of Foreign Affairs, resigned from his post, and, not unlike 1982 when he had joined forces with Mr. Compton to oust a discredited SLP government, in 2001 Mr. Odlum again teamed up with the then retired Sir John Compton to form a political alliance with which they hoped to successfully contest the next general elections and then introduce a government of national unity. In that alliance, a group of concerned citizens appointed Mr. Odlum political leader, Sir John, president and Dr. Morella Joseph (leader of the UWP), vice president. So just as Mr. Odlum had flirted with history back in 1979 when he had introduced a new brand of politics and had attempted a new style of government, with this promise of a government of national unity he was again flirting with history, for he was attempting to navigate a course that went against the path set by precedence. However, besides these noble ideals, one sensed that Mr. Odlum had some personal reasons for ditching the Labor Party.

Wary of his left of center ideology and recognizing his prominent role in the fall of the 1979 Labor Government, the 1997 SLP Government had gone to great pains to ensure that Mr. Odlum had only a very marginal role in the internal workings of the Party and the government. So much so, that between Mr. Odlum and the Prime Minister there were two deputy Prime Ministers. So, above all other reasons, it was probably this ostracism that caused Mr. Odlum to rebel against his Party.

For his part, Sir John conceded that the government had made a shamble of the economy in general and the banana industry in particular. He said that many businesses and well-respected citizens had come to him with the suggestion of forming an alliance to save the country from what they called the economic mismanagement of the Dr. Kenny Anthony led Labor government. Yet one could well imagine that in Sir John Compton's mind this new alliance would serve the same purpose as the PLP and the National Labor Movement Party alliance (nearly four decades before) that had provided him the vehicle with which to dominate the country's politics for three decades. Still, one could not help but suspect that another reason Sir John felt compelled to come out of retirement was to protect his legacy, which, since the SLP had attained power, had been under constant verbal attack.

Nevertheless, just when the Alliance had gained

national acceptance and momentum and was seen as a se-rious threat to the Labor Party's rule come next elections (and in the eyes of many, represented the country's only hope of removing Dr. Kenny Anthony and his Labor Party from power), a leadership struggle developed between Mr. Odlum and Mr. Compton.

Mr. Odlum accused Mr. Comption of an unwillingness or inability to subordinate himself to anyone. And Mr. Compton protested Mr. Odlum's close ties with Libya's Muammar al-Qaddafi and the potential harm that these ties could bring to St. Lucia.

At a National Alliance Assembly, which Mr. Odlum chose not to attend, Mr. Compton was unanimously elected political leader of the Party. Mr. Odlum denounced this new election as illegitimate and insisted that he was the political leader of the Party. Exasperated with the rivalry between the two men, and concluding that they were causing more harm than good, Dr. Morella Joseph divorced her United Workers Party from the Alliance and proceeded to prepare her Party for general elections. But refusing to give in to history, Mr. Odlum forged ahead with the much weaker and smaller National Alliance Party, of which he became the undisputed political leader. On the other hand, bowing to history, Mr. Compton threw his support behind Dr. Morella Joseph and the UWP.

General elections were due in May 2002, yet the

once formidable Labor Party that had come to power with an enviable 16 - 1 majority was now on shaky ground because of a failing economy due largely to a weakening tourism sector and a banana industry in shambles.

The UWP, historically a well-organized and functioning Party, was in disarray and its breakup with the Alliance had left it scrambling to regroup.

The National Alliance, which was never on solid ground to begin with, was sinking. The leadership struggle and the subsequent withdrawal of the UWP had caused people to lose faith in the Party. More so because this was the very same Party that was preaching government of national unity. Furthermore, without the UWP the National Alliance didn't have the necessary machinery with which to seriously contest a general election.

Recognizing its predicament of a weak economy, the Labor Party was quick to capitalize on the unpreparedness of the National Alliance and the UWP. It called early elections for December 3, 2001.

Two other parties, the Staff Party and the Freedom Party, joined the fight. But in the eyes of the public they were just protest parties and of little consequence in these elections.

The polls proved that the Labor Party had gambled correctly. The unpreparedness and disarray of the Alli-

ance and the UWP were too great to defeat a well-organized and functioning Labor Party, even one facing a failing economy. On December 3, 2001, the St. Lucia Labor
Party returned to power with a 14 - 3 majority, making it
the second consecutive elections that the Party had won
by a landslide, and thus leaving one to wonder whether
the party's 1979 dream of a one-Party state had finally
become a reality.

Regarding dreams, Mr. Odlum's Alliance won not
one seat, (the UWP winning all three opposition seats),
so once again Mr. Odlum was unable to defeat history.

Again, paying little attention to history, but plenty
of attention to politics and prices, some farmers
abandoned their fields altogether. Many, as if
revolting against the constant demands of the banana,
for once allowed the fruit to take care of itself, visiting
their fields only to harvest what bunches the banana
plants had decided to cough up. Neglected, diseases
such as leaf spot took over, turning once bluish-green,
vigorous fields into sick, brownish-yellow fields begging
in vain for care and attention. The Roseau Valley, the
valley that the UWP government had bought from Geest
in 1982 and then divided into model farms owned by
the workers themselves, which in the eighties yielded
fifteen to twenty tonnes of bananas per acre, was
reduced to only five or six tonnes per acre. And as if all

this weren't enough, the island was hit with what many considered the worst drought in 40 years. So for most of 2001, all around the island bananas and the soil that provided them sustenance looked sick and exhausted, as if to say they had had enough.

16

Tourism: Savior Or Curse?

Another possible reason why the nation had not paid much attention to farmers' demands was that, although bananas still formed a major component of the economy, by 1993 tourism had grown to the point of being able to challenge its supremacy, not unlike the way bananas had come up against sugar in the 1950's.

Before 1965 there was virtually no tourism industry in St. Lucia. But with a government willing to go to great lengths (generous incentive packages that included tax exemptions and access to the best beaches) to reduce the country's over reliance on bananas, the tourism industry was soon to take off. And fortunately for the country it did so in the 1970's just when beaten down by droughts the banana industry began to falter.

The immediate contribution of the tourism sector, however, wasn't the tourist dollar but the construction boom that it caused. Halcyon Days came to Vieux Fort in 1969. In Castries (Rodney Bay and Gros Islet) St. Lucia Beach Hotel renamed Rex St. Lucian Hotel came around 1960, Club St. Lucia in 1967, Islander Hotel in 1980, Rendezvous in 1981, Windjammer Landing in 1989, Marlin Quay and Royal St. Lucia in 1991, Windjammer Morgan Bay in 1992, Orange Grove and Caribbees Hotel in 1993, Sandals Halcyon in 1994, Bay Gardens in 1995, the Hyatt in 2000. In Soufrière Anse Chastanet came in 1968, Ladera Resort in 1970, Jalousie Hilton in 1992.

Suddenly, instead of a few visitors who were on the island mostly as consultants and volunteer workers, crowds of tourists could be seen in Castries and to a lesser extent Soufrière and Vieux Fort, hugging beaches and strolling along the island's streets. Such was the stir caused by these hotels that many farmers abandoned their bananas and rural settings and migrated to Castries (especially) to share in the tourism bounty.

The construction boom that tourism set off was just the beginning. By 1986 the island could boast of 1,826 guest house and hotel rooms, accommodating 3599 beds. In that year visitor arrivals, not including cruise passengers, totaled 115,472, and tourist expenditures reached EC$184 million. So rapid was the growth in tourism that the contribution of tourism to GDP had increased manifold from EC$2.2 million in 1970 to EC$54 million in 1986.

In the early 1990's, after a decade of unprecedented growth, bananas started its decline. But tourism did not falter. So much so that by 1991, two years before the banana strike, with an estimated hotel and guest house capacity of 3028 rooms, tourism expenditures of EC$470 million, stay-over visitor arrivals surpassing the island's population, and 318 cruise ships calling at port with 153 thousand visitors, the tourism sector eclipsed the banana industry, and probably for good. In that year compared with bananas' GDP contributions of EC$81.5 million, or 8.6 percent of GDP, tourism contributed EC$105 million, representing 10.3 percent of GDP.

And by the year 2000, the number of tourist stay-overs had surpassed the 260 thousand mark, and cruise ship passengers were numbering in the 400 thousands. Tourism's EC$219 million contribution to real GDP was almost four times that of bananas and nearly twice that of the whole agricultural sector.

Encouraged no doubt by these statistics and proba-bly also by the observation that many of the more afflu-

ent Caribbean islands were those with the most developed tourism industry (Barbados, Antigua, Bahamas, for
example), in the year 2001 the Prime Minister, a law
professor, not a farmer, proclaimed to the whole nation,
as if they themselves were not yet aware of the fact,
that banana was no longer klng. From that pronounce-
ment and from his previous year's budget speech it was
clear that the Prime Minister was in no doubt that
tourism in particular and the service sector in general
was now king. First it had been sugar, then banana took
its turn, and now in the same way that the Prime
Minister, a law professor, not a farmer, had replaced Sir
John Compton, himself a banana farmer, tourism had
now dethroned bananas.

Like bananas, the changes brought about by the
tourism industry went beyond economics.   Beautiful
luxurious hotels came to occupy beaches that the population once considered largely inaccessible and of little
aesthetic value. One steps out of the tropical heat, and
the unstructured, "everything goes," "don't dig nothing," "no problem man" climate of the island, walks
through hanging gardens and well-manicured hotel
grounds, and then enters well polished, soft lighting and
air-conditioned hotel lobbies where van Gogh paintings
greet the eye. The overwhelming impression is that
suddenly the Third World has been exchanged for the
Developed World, where in sharp contrast to the rest of

the island, things work the way they were designed to work, the way they were supposed to work, and where beautiful young ladies dress, groom and speak beautifully for the tourists. So sweet and polished are their accents that they would no doubt sound foreign to the rest of the Third Worldish St. Lucian population.

With the coming of tourism many things have acquired greater importance and have been given more serious attention. In fact, attention and respect that farmers and the banana industry never received tourists and the tourism industry were receiving in great abundance. The tourist needed to know where they were going, so soon green and white roadway signs appeared around the island, and city, town and village streets that existed for years without (visible) names were given names for all to see. "In view of the tourism industry," proclaimed the Vieux Fort Town Clerk, "thirty-nine street signs will resurrect in Vieux Fort." The tourists needed comfort and surroundings that pleased the eye, so street cleaning, roadway maintenance and landscaping, and proper garbage disposal took urgent importance. The tourists needed to feel safe and secure, because however beautiful and sunny the island, they could not enjoy their vacation amid fear and distrust. So crime fighting, especially in the areas tourists most frequented, became an overnight national priority. For example, a special rapid response police unit was established at Rodney Bay, arguably the capital of St. Lucia's tourism sector. In brief, the tourists needed to walk on clean, safe, well paved, beautifully adorned streets with visible names, along which were happy locals smiling them "good morning." To ensure that the locals got the picture, school children were entered into prize winning essay contests on the benefits of tourism to St. Lucia, something bananas never heard of. Leaving nothing to chance, and to make sure no one tarnished the image: *Simply Beautiful*, by print, radio and television the population were educated about the importance of the tourist's dollar, on how to treat the tourists, how to make their stay as comfortable and enjoyable as possible, so that they would come back again and again. After all, the job of tourism was the responsibility of not just the hotels but the whole population. To crown it all, the Par Excellence Award Ceremony, the most glamorous and prestigious event of its kind in St. Lucia, was instituted to make sure that those who advanced the tourism industry were lifted to the apex of national adulation.

There were still more changes. Estates in decline were resuscitated into botanical gardens for the distinct pleasure of the tourist. Historical sites that to the local eye held no value, because many had refused to accept that the island has a history worth bothering with (for example, in St. Lucia it is no longer compulsory for secondary school students to take history as a subject), suddenly became national treasures, because in the eyes of the tourist they were sites to behold. Waterfalls, once too insignificant to be noticed, became postcards and the covers of magazines. Rastafarians and street bums, previously lacking occupation and livelihood, became artists, self-appointed cultural ambassadors and tour guides. Dissatisfied with the island's Third World service and keeping true to their all-inclusiveness, the hotels established their own police force, in the process creating nations within nations. Fire eating, belly and limbo dancers, not to be found in the country's cultural archives, sprang up overnight to keep the visitors entertained with the island's culture. In the year 2000 the government legitimatized casino gambling, not for the locals, but to ensure that the tourist didn't get too bored with the island's abundance of sun, beach, mountains, sky and beautiful smiles. But for the outcry of environmentalists and of Mr. Derek Walcott, St. Lucia's very own literature Nobel Laureate, the Pitons, sacred gods of the Caribs, would have been decapitated to provide tourists rides on aerial tramcars. In the 1950's a banana culture began replacing a sugar plantation slave culture, but beginning in the 1970s and getting into full swing in the 1990s a tourist culture began replacing the banana culture, forcing a poet to remark:"*they are here again, instead of sugar and plantations they have come for sunshine and beaches, the hotel workers have traded places with the field slaves, the government with the overseer, only this time it is voluntary enslavement."*

Like bananas, tourism came with its own set of baggage. As developed islands in a Third World Ocean, the hotels represent the most affluent pieces of the island. This along with the fact that most of the guests are Caucasians as opposed to the clear majority of the population who are of African and Asian descent, has created, as exist in America, a dual society that gives the appearance that everything white is superior to everything black. The emphasis and priority that the government in particular and the country in general have been giving to the needs of the tourists further enhance that perception because they appear to be saying that the tourists are more important and of greater value than the citizens of the country.

However beautiful the hotels, it takes real bravery for non-white St. Lucians, no matter their income and education, to enter. The smiles of the beautifully groomed young ladies, and their sweetly polished accents are only for the tourist, and most of the tourists are white. Despite the well-known fact that all the beaches in the country are by law freely available to all its citizens, it takes some bravery to walk the beaches fronting the hotels. Because not only does one have to sidestep braless, suntanning tourists, but the eyes of the stationed police force within a police force seem to say loudly and clearly that the law may say that you have clear access to the beach, but don't fool yourself, in reality this beach here is for the tourists, and a tourist is a white person. So naturally, as soon as a hotel appears near some beach, the local population shies away. The presence of the hotel proving more effective than legislation denying access to the beaches. Moreover, some hotels are so situated that the only access to the beach is through their properties, which means passing through security check points. All this suggests that every new hotel, every additional tourist gracing the population with their presence signal yet another piece of sovereignty lost.

Some argue that even in the developed world governments go all out to attract tourists, so why should a Third World country like St. Lucia, a country that needs tourism much more than the developed countries, have problems with tourism. To respond to that argument, several important differences between tourism in, say the United States and St. Lucia, should be noted. Firstly, in the United States many of the tourists look no different than the greater majority of the population. Secondly, the tourists enjoy a similar level of affluence in their home country as do many American citizens. Thirdly, even if millions of tourists visit the United States each year, they still form a fraction of the nearly 300 million people who reside in the US. In St. Lucia, on the other hand, not only do most of the tourists look different from most of the citizenry, but they enjoy a greater level of affluence in their home country than do most St. Lucians, and the annual number of stay-over visitors alone, not to mention cruise ship visitors that by the year 2000 had exceeded 400 thousand, is greater than the island's population. So clearly, in the St. Lucian scenario, the social and cultural destabilizing effects of tourism would be greater, and the competition between tourists and the citizenry for scarce resources would be more intense.

Nevertheless, it would be misleading not to point out that for a small country like St. Lucia the presence of a viable tourism sector helps to provide the critical mass that makes possible many activities and spheres of endeavor that otherwise (due to limited market and population) would be economically unviable. The additional demand and market the tourist sector represents enables utility companies and other service providers to operate at more economical scales of operations. Farmers and fishermen are presented with a market that is probably more stable and more reliable than the local non-hotel market. Without the hotels, many musicians, entertainers, artistes, and crafts-persons probably could not have depended full-time on their creativity for a living. Without tourism, events such as the St. Lucian Jazz Festival, touted as the second best in the world, the

Carnival Parade, the Calypso Finals, and Jouné Kwéyòl would not have achieved the scale that they have acquired. In fact, without tourism the Jazz Festival may not have been at all possible.

Still, as with bananas and with sugar before bananas, with tourism the country is in danger of over-relying on a single economic activity. The danger is even more perilous considering the fickleness of tourism. Any of several factors can undermine the tourism industry—economic downturns in the developed world, an outside perception of rising crime and political instability, other tourist destinations becoming more fashionable than the Caribbean. Even the island's hurricanes, the nemesis of the banana industry, can cripple the tourism industry in any given year. The setback that the September 11, 2001 World Trade Center assault brought to the tourism sector is but a case in point.

The worldwide trend of the tourism industry becoming increasingly dominated by all-inclusive hotels and cruise tourists further exacerbates the perils of becoming over-dependent on the tourism industry. It is well acknowledged that a large percentage of the tourist dollar never enters the hands of the citizens of host countries like St. Lucia, but remains in the home countries of the airline companies, travel agents and hotel owners. So much so, that in spite of the employment opportunities tourism bring, a study by economist, Brian

Copeland, suggests that without heavy taxes on the domestic services and resources that the tourists use intensively, the net welfare gains from an expansion of tourism could be negligible or even negative. With cruise ship visitors and all inclusive hotels this has become even more so because not only do these visitors spend less money in the host country but with these hotels less of what the visitors spend gets circulated in the host economy. In fact, it seems that the inclusive hotels are designed for the tourist to interact minimally with their host countries, and to spend as little time and money as possible outside the hotels.

17

The St. Lucia Renaissance

If there was one area and period in which the island's inhabitants had circumvented history, or, at the very least, put history to work to their advantage, it would have to be in art and culture during the 1950 to 1971 period, when the St. Lucia Arts Guild unleashed the greatest outpouring of St. Lucian artistic creativity the island has ever seen. Among its more notable exponents were novelist Garth St. Omer, playwright Roderick Walcott, painter Dustan St. Omer, and poet, playwright and Nobel Laureate Derek Walcott. The twenty-year period (1950-1971) that the Arts Guild span could certainly be a candidate for the golden era of St. Lucian art and literature, and can be aptly described as the St. Lucia Renaissance, for arguably up till today these above-mentioned exponents of the Arts Guild have remained unmatched in St. Lucia in their respective fields of artistic endeavor.

How did the St. Lucia Renaissance happen? What were the forces that brought it about? Well, to find answers to these questions, we need to go back into history.

The British West Indies Federation lasted only four years, 1958 to 1962, yet the very notion of a federation, much less its implementation, had inspired a people and lifted their hopes, aspirations, and creative spirit to unprecedented heights. So, in investigating the St. Lucia renaissance, it may be instructive to explore the events and forces that led to the Federation, and what about the spirit of the Federation that inspired a nation, a civilization, to artistic greatness. Before the Federation and up to the early 1900's, West Indians had been more or less contented to being part of the British Empire, and who could blame them. By 1900 the British King, Edward VII, reigned over 410 million people and his dominion stretched across 11.4 million square miles, making the British Empire the largest the world had ever known. Clearly, if there were one empire to choose to belong to, it would have had to be the British Empire. In fact, not only were West Indians pleased to be under British rule, but culturally the striving was to become English ladies and gentlemen. After all, there was great value in modeling oneself after the British. To be English was to be cultured. Moreover, white plantation owners together with their surrogates in government ruled the land. Most of the civil service jobs and the choice positions at commercial houses were reserved for their offspring. Exclusive social clubs for whites only cemented their control over the economic life of the territories. Therefore, the closer to being British (if not in color at least in mannerism and culture) one became, the better were one's chances of sharing in the wealth of the homeland. However, soon after the opening of the 20th century, events and circumstances started unfolding that would open cracks in this West Indian coziness with and allegiance to the British Empire.

In 1902 the Americans bought the failed Panama Canal enterprise from the French for US$40 million, and by 1905 work had begun on the Canal in earnest. Roughly 50,000 West Indians emigrated to Panama to work on the Canal and as such they were to play an important role as agents of change in West Indian society.

In Panama, not only did West Indian workers receive a baptism in labor-capital confrontations, an experience they would later put to good use in the Caribbean, but besides exposure to American notions of rugged individualism and disregard for class distinctions, they came face to face with the American style of racism. The Canal was completed in 1914, and the West Indians who returned home arrived with a new concept of self. Dressed in flashy clothes and jewelry, they exuded self-confidence and self-importance. No doubt, these outward signs of the good life displayed by people who not too long before were no different than the rest of the population, must have fueled the imagination and expectations of those who had stayed behind of what could be had, not just in terms of luxuries but in terms of education and self-actualization.

The Panama Canal workers influenced West Indian societies in other ways. Some used their Panama money to educate their children, thus giving rise to a new generation of professionals of working class parents. Others having been schooled in the labor confrontations of the Panama Canal, and who after their Panama money ran out found themselves on the unemployment roll, became the vanguard of the West Indian labor movements of the 1930' and 40's.

As the Panama Canal came to completion, World War I came along, and with a great sense of patriotism and duty West Indians welcomed the opportunity to fight in defense of the motherland and its empire. From

Jamaica alone, more than 10,000 volunteers enlisted in the British military. Altogether more than 16,000 West Indian soldiers served under the British flag. In terms of a military power, West Indians would have been hard pressed to do better than Britain. At the outset of the war, Britain's 442 warships made its Royal Navy by far the most powerful in the world. So one could well imagine the shock these black British soldiers suffered when once in the field they realized that no matter their training, education, talent, zeal and patriotism they were deemed inferior to troops from other parts of the British hegemony, including Canada, Australia, and New Zealand, and good only for the most menial of tasks. It didn't help that the West Indians observed that both the Americans and the French were treating their black soldiers with greater respect than the British were treating them.

And if all these weren't enough for the West Indian soldiers to get the message that race mattered, and that as long as they remained black or nonwhite they would never acquire full membership into the British empire, the news that must have filtered down from the United States to the West Indies, that more than 70 blacks were lynched in the year after the war ended, and that several black soldiers still in army uniform were among the lynched, would have definitely brought home the point, particularly since the performance and bravery of the 200,000 African American soldiers who served in Europe were legendary. For example, the American 369th Regiment of which many were African Americans were the first soldiers to break through the German lines to reach the Rhine, and during 191 days of fighting the regiment didn't have a man captured, nor did it lose an inch of ground. Out of respect for the fighting spirit of the African Americans (not unlike the fierce fighting spirit of the buffalo soldiers of the US 10th Calvary Regiment in the Indian Wars) the Germans renamed them the hell fighters, and so impressed was the French Army that it honored the 369th regiment with the Croix de Guerre.

West Indian participation in World War I brought home other lessons. The War marked a period of industrial and political upheaval in Russia. In the October 1917 Russian Revolution, Tsar Nicholas II was forced to relinquish his reign. Lenin was ushered into power and thus began the transformation of Russia from a feudal-capitalist system to a communist state. Since Russia was fighting on the same side as Britain, the War brought West Indian soldiers in contact with Marxism and Russian nationalism. Ideas and sensibilities, which after the humiliation suffered at the hands of their British superiors, they had definitely become much more receptive and sympathetic to, and which no doubt made them question and reexamine their own situation back home and their relations with empire. Clearly, the seeds of

West Indian Federation as a breaking away from Britain had been planted. Consider, for example, that it was World War I veterans like Tubal Uriah "Buzz" Butler and Arthur Andrew Cipriani who were at the forefront of Trinidad's labor movement (Khan), and consider also Clennell Wickham, another veteran who after the War, in 1919, founded The Barbados Herald, a radical and cultural activist weekly newspaper.

Another crack would soon appear in West Indians' cozy relationship with Britain. Italy's fascist dictator, Benito Mussolini, came to power in 1922 with grand designs of returning Italy to the glory days of the Roman Empire. In 1936 Italy invaded Abyssinia, better known as Ethiopia. Despite having an overwhelmingly military superiority, Italy used poison gas on their adversary, extinguishing all life over large areas of the country. Italy conquered Abyssinia. The title of emperor of Abyssinia was taken over by the Italian King, Emanuel III. Emperor Hail Selassie fled to England and did not return until six years later in 1941, when the Italian army was defeated in East Africa during World War II. The fact that Britain, the world's super power, had not come to the aid of Ethiopia was a source of great disgust to West Indians who saw this as nothing less than a betrayal of the black race.

Yet, if by then West Indians, like the striking banana famers, were not taking heed of history, and so were not totally convinced that this empire business wasn't working for them, the events of the 1930's (coinciding with the Great Depression and plummeting sugar prices) of extreme poverty, deplorable working conditions, labor uprisings that unleashed British warships and police firing squads on protestors, would have definitely done the trick.

Under this onslaught, the cozy relationship that once existed between Britain and its West Indian subjects was shattered. The West Indies was in a state of agitation and unrest. Labor Unions followed by political parties sprang up overnight. The George Charles led St. Lucia Workers Cooperative Union turned into the St. Lucia Labor Party. In this state of social, political and economic crisis, West Indian Federation became an increasingly attractive proposition.

Crisis forces change and paradigm shifts. West Indian society found itself at a crossroad. The people had arrived at a point where they could no longer deny history, deny that they were not British and that they could never be British. If they were not British, they had to be West Indian. But what did it mean to be a West Indian? Clearly, in this period West Indians began an earnest quest of self-discovery and self-definition. They began the cultivation of a West Indian identity as distinct from their African or Asian roots and their colonial heritage.

All this internal examination and discovery found

ultimate expression in the notion of a West Indian Federation, such that for once West Indians were willing and able to put aside race, class and territorial barriers and buy into the concept of regional unity. For once the idealism of regional identity transcended all else.

In his poem, *A Far Cry from Africa*, Derek Walcott gave voice to the West Indian dilemma of being caught between two loyalties—that of empire and one's original heritage, be it African or Asian. He said:

Where shall I turn, divided to the vein?
I who have cursed
The drunken officer of British rule, how choose
Between this Africa and the English tongue I love?
Betray them both, or give them back what they give?

In hindsight, how has West Indians answered Walcott? It appears that West Indians have not so much as rejected Europe or Africa or Asia, as they have embraced a West Indian identity that may reflect both inheritances yet represents something new and different. And apparently this excruciating process of finding themselves, of discovering who they are, of consciously becoming West Indian, began in the crucible period of the 1930's through to the early 1960's, and unleashed the region's (not just St. Lucia) greatest outpouring of art and culture and creativity.

Sir Derek Walcott

For example, of the ten authors whom a 1995 survey of West Indian literature, edited by Bruce King, classified as significant West Indian authors, the region's literary giants, seven were either born in the early 1930's or came of age in the labor and political upheavals of the late 1930's. These authors include Wilson Harris of Guyana, Samuel Selvon, Earl Lovelace and V.S. Naipaul of

Trinidad and Tobago, George Lamming and Edward Kamau Brathwaite of Barbados, and Derek Walcott of St. Lucia. Two of these significant authors—Derek Walcott and V.S. Naipaul—have since won the Nobel Prize for literature, and a few like Wilson Harris were knocking on the door.

In another survey, The West Indian Novel and its Background, Kenneth Ramchand found that about fifty-five novels were published between 1949 and 1959 by twenty different authors. The poets were also active. In this period, Derek Walcott published his first three volumes of poetry; and others, including Edward Kamau Brathwaite, Martin Carter, Frank Collymore and E.M. Roach also added their voices.

Similarly, according to Caribbean Literature lecturer, Sandra Pouchet Paquet, this period also saw an upswing in drama, painting and sculpture; and the establishment of several institutions providing support for the arts, including the University College of the West Indies (renamed the University of the West Indies), the Little Carib Dance Company in Trinidad, the Jamaican School of Arts and Crafts, and the National Dance Theatre Company of Jamaica. Likewise, literary magazines like Guyana's *Kyk-over-al* and Barbados's *Bim* were in full swing, facilitating the exchange of ideas among West Indian artists and intellectuals. And in St. Lucia, defeating history, the St. Lucia Arts Guild, established in 1950, would set off a cultural and artistic renaissance.

In this turbulent era, the demand for national freedom and self-determination was by no means limited to the Caribbean. In fact, it was a worldwide phenomenon. By 1947, the Indian subcontinent had fought and won their independence. Starting in the fifties, the African continent had begun their independent march. Their cry for freedom and "Africa for Africans" could be heard loud and clear, such that between the Second World War and the start of the West Indian Federation, seven African countries had gained their independence, including the British ruled nations of Egypt, Sudan and Ghana. In 1957, the Fidel Castro-led Cuban revolution had claimed Cuba for the Cuban people. In America, in 1955, the Civil Rights Movement had begun in earnest. Martin Luther King's famous "I Have A Dream" speech was only eight years away; and soon Malcolm X would start sewing his seeds of armed self-defense and black nationalism that would germinate into the Black Panther and Black Power Movements. Clearly, all these events would have inspired and spurred on West Indians in their struggle for self-determination.

The West Indian Federation came to an end in 1962, and dashed the hopes and aspirations of a civilization. Professionals and intellectuals who had remained home specifically to contribute to the development of the region packed up and left. Those in England and America

Sir Dunstan St. Omer

who were in the process of making plans to return home to play their part in civilization building stayed put. Literary magazines like Guyana's *Kyk-over-al,* whose founding had been inspired by the mere notion of a West Indian Federation, went out of press. Novelists, poets, dramatists, painters, all took turns lashing out at the politicians for their selfishness and shortsightedness.

And, not unlike the ethnic tensions and chaos that accompanied the breakup of the Soviet Empire, following the demise of the Federation, West Indian civilization began cracking up, returning to its pre-federation rivalry and conflicts. In 1962, a bloody civil war along political and racial lines (Blacks versus Indians), flared up in Guyana, claiming hundreds of lives. The larger West Indian territories (larger, if not in size at least in population), including Jamaica, Trinidad, Barbados and Guyana, gained their independence from Britain, thus setting up a dichotomy in the region that fueled national chauvinism, where the independent countries thought of themselves as superior to their tinier neighbors. And according to Caribbean and women literature lecturer, Rhonda Cobham, after the collapse of the federation the "fragile regional alliance between the professional middle class and the working class against the common colonial enemy was swept away by a new wave of elitism."

But by then, in terms of art and culture, in terms of self-realization and self-discovery, in terms of coming to grips with what it meant to be a West Indian, in terms of helping to foster a distinct Caribbean art, theatre, and literature, in terms of motivating the establishment of organs and institutions that would enable art and cultural expressions to continue to flourish, the federation had done its job.

For its part, during this West Indian civilization building period, St. Lucia fought a revolution on three fronts. On one front, there was George Charles, John Compton and their compatriots fighting for workers' rights, fight-

Harold F Simmons

ing for self-rule, fighting for political and territorial liberation. On the second front, bananas took over from sugar as the island's leading economic activity, in the process empowering the people economically and setting off an economic and social revolution. And on the third front, there was Derek Walcott, Roderick Walcott, Dunstan St. Omer and the other members of the St. Lucia Arts Guild fighting for the hearts, minds, and souls of St. Lucians; fighting to free the St. Lucian psyche from, as Bob Marley said, "mental slavery," fighting to decapitate the notion that provincial means inferior, that the island's folk creole culture wasn't worthy of art and celebration, and that black wasn't beautiful.

Of these three revolutionary fronts, the cultural renaissance has probably received the least attention (Woe be unto those who are unmindful of history) but it was probably the most remarkable of the three and it was what set St. Lucia most apart from its Caribbean neighbors.

Dunstan St. Omer, considered the father of St. Lucian painting and as such a cultural hero, harbors no doubt about what motivated the St. Lucia Arts Guild outburst of creative energy and hence the renaissance. He said, "It was a time in history when the world was changing. The whole world was moving towards independence and self-determination, the breakdown of colonialism and imperialism." He went further to explain that part of the reason for forming the Arts Guild was to rid St. Lucians of their inferiority complexes. "The black boys (of the Arts Guild) were up, recreating their society, kicking out the Victorian society that overlaid the country."

For example, he said that in those days "it was forbidden" to speak patio in schools, then "Derek with his genius" started writing poems and plays peppered with St. Lucian patio and in which he was using the syntax of patois, thereby creolizing his writings, "and patio became legitimate, in the process giving the people back their language, and in the process giving them their self-confidence, in doing that they found their equality. Because as long as you using another man's thing you are not equal, but when you doing your own thing, you are yourself. You are equal."

The Arts Guild did more than uplift the St. Lucian spirit. According to St. Omer, it started a revolution in West Indian theatre. "We open the West Indian dramatic mind. Everybody was paying tribute to us for that. At this time St. Lucia was leading the way in West Indian theatre. The rest of the Caribbean caught the bug of being local, of being original. It influenced a cultural revolution across the entire Caribbean."

Henri Christophe, a play about the Haitian Revolution, was one of Derek Walcott's first plays and one of the first plays staged by the St. Lucia Arts Guild. A critic reviewing for the *West India Committee Circular* the 1952 London production of *Henri Christophe*, in which all the actors were West Indians residing in Britain, seemed to agree with Dunstan St. Omer. He wrote, "In the development of an indigenous culture in the Caribbean (and no West Indian Federation can really be without it) no element is of greater potential importance than a West Indian theatre, for the theatre is the meeting place and the nursery of the arts. At the same time the initial obstacles are formidable. The three essential elements in the theatre—the playwright, the actor and the audience—must exist together if the theatre is to be a living reality in the life of the people. This condition has not hitherto existed in the West Indies. ... There have certainly been writers, actors and audiences in the West Indies in the past, but not West Indian writers of West Indian plays for West Indian actors to perform to West Indian audiences. ... In this critical stage of development of a West Indian theatre, the recent production of *Henri Christophe* ... is an event of the first importance. It was in every way a West Indian production."

According to Kendel Hippolyte, St. Lucian poet and playwright, during the period of the St. Lucia Arts Guild (1950 to 1971), the Guild staged no less than sixty-one plays. Twenty of these plays were by St. Lucians, and seven were by other Caribbean writers. Several members of the Guild, including Derek and Roderick Walcott, Allan Weekes, Howick Elcock, Eric Branford, Garth St. Omer and George Odlum, took turns directing these plays.

Of the twenty plays by St. Lucian writers, ten were

Roderick Walcott

by Roderick Walcott: *The Harrowing of Benjy, Shrove Tuesday March, The One Eye is King, A Flight of Sparrows, Malfinis, The Education of Alfie, The Banjo Man, The Devil at Christmas, The Trouble with Albino Joe,* and *The Expatriates*; Five were by Derek Walcott: *Henri Christophe, The Sea at Dauphin, Ti Jean and his Brothers, Malcochon,* and *Jourmand;* Two were by Irvin Grey: *The Serenaders,* and *The Bitter Seed*; Another two were by Stanley French: *The Rape of Fair Helen* and *The Ballad of a Man and Dog*; And one was by Allan Weekes: *Talk of the Devil.*

At this point it would be a glaring omission if this account did not invoke the memory of Harold Fitzgerald Simmons, for though, regarding the St. Lucia Arts Guild, he was only in the background, by most accounts he planted the seed of the St. Lucia Renaissance. Indeed, behind any discussion or initiative on St. Lucia art and culture, or the awarding of any prize to St. Lucian nationals for their work in that field of endeavor, looms the singular, solitary figure of Harold Simmons (1914-1966), for he is considered not just the father of the St. Lucia Arts Guild and hence the St. Lucia Renaissance but the father of St. Lucian Culture.

Born on December 2, 1914, sixteen years ahead of the Walcott brothers, Harold Simmons was a local historian, archaeologist, artist (painter), journalist, folklorist and social worker. To illustrate the pivotal role of Simmons in the shaping of the artistic sensibilities of the Arts Guild, consider that, according to St. Omer, it was only upon meeting Simmons as a teenager and spending time in Simmons' art studio that he learned "art (painting) is on the level of poetry and philosophy."

Now, it isn't that the aspiring artist wasn't doing his homework. He used to spend hours in the Castries

Central Library studying art books, familiarizing himself with the works of the European masters. But all along he was under the misconception that art was only what was in those books, and anything outside those books wasn't art. So being an artist simply meant reproducing the works of the masters.

Looking back, St. Omer said he wasn't surprised that he had formed such an impression of art. Because after all this was the colonial era, "where all the values were colonial values," and everything else was considered inferior, vulgar, uncultured. In sharp contrast to St. Omer's notion of art, Harry Simmons told his protégés (Walcott and St. Omer) to "paint what you see, paint what was around you, paint what was yours."

St. Omer said that Harry made them "see that follow-ing the European thing was mere imitation." Their encounter with Simmons represented the first time they were meeting a real artist, a professional painter, work-ing in a real studio, and also the first time they were see-ing paintings of St. Lucian scenes: coconut trees, fisher-men with their canoes, country folk, madrases, St. Lucian heroes. "Suddenly," said St. Omer, "in Harry's studio St. Lucia became art."

Despite being such an eye opener to his students, both Derek and Dunstan admitted that Simmons didn't so much as teach them techniques or how to paint, but it was the example that he represented and their reorientation to the meaning and purpose of art that left a lasting impression on them. Here is Derek Walcott on the subject. "The influence was not so much technical. Of course, I picked up a few things from him in terms of technique: how to do a good sky, how to water the paper, how to circle it, how to draw properly and concentrate on it, and all of that. But there were other things apart from the drawing. Mostly, it was the model of the man as a professional artist that was the example."

So Simmons didn't teach his charges how to paint, but what he taught them couldn't be found in text books or structured art classes. He unleashed the imagination and channeled the talent and creativity of his protégés toward what was inside them and what was their own. He set them off on an epic journey of self-discovery, on a pilgrimage to claim for themselves and their people what was rightfully theirs. He gave them new pairs of eyes with which to see their country and behold their people. And what they saw and beheld was amazing beauty no less deserving of theatre, of music, of poetry, of paintings, of dance, of novels than any other. Simmons did nothing less than liberate the St. Lucian souls of his protégés and set these souls soaring.

Upon Simmons death, Derek Walcott wrote, "He was one of the first water colorists the West Indies has produced" and he helped to "create a community of writers

Dr. Garth St. Omer

and painters among whom were Sybil Atteck and Edgar Mittleholzer... For us he was like a walking museum that contained knowledge of all styles and our first paintings slavishly imitated his ... Because of him we could not have been anything else, and whatever honor his former pupils gain are homage to his spirit."

Clearly, unlike the banana famers, the members of the St. Lucia Arts Guild paid homage to history, Walcott and St. Omer in particular, and they conquered the world.

Aglance at the achievements and body of work of the more outstanding members of the Arts Guild may help put the accomplishments of the Guild in perspective. As a playwright, Stanley French (1937-2010) published five plays: *The Rape of Fair Helen* (1983), *His Light and the Dark, Ballad of a Man and Dog, The Interview, No Rain No Play,* and *Under a Sky of Incense* (1977). Besides St. Lucia, his plays have been staged in London, Nigeria, and the Caribbean—most notably Jamaica. Stanley French was also a sports writer. His writings on cricket were published in the collections: *Francis Mindoo Phillip: A Portrait from Memory* (1979), and *Come In, My Lords, Come In!* (2004). In 2000 he was awarded Saint Lucia Gold Medal of Merit (2000) for his contributions to the literary and performing arts.

A generation younger than the Walcotts, McDonald Dixon (1944 —) joined the Arts Guild during its later years so he may be more aptly grouped with the next or second generation of artists who were inspired by and came immediately after the Arts Guild. He hasn't received the kind of international attention that some of the other members of the Arts Guild have received, but as a playwright, poet, novelist and photographer he stands out among the second generation of artists. Besides writing and directing a number of critically acclaimed plays, he has published three novels: *Season of Mist* (2000), *Misbegotten* (2009), *Saints of Little Paradise: Book One 'eden Defiled'* (2012); a collection of short stories: *Careme and other Stories* (2009), and several volumes of poetry most of which reprinted in his latest collection, *Collected Poems 1961-2001* (2003). In 1993 he was awarded St. Lucia Medal of Merit (Silver) for his contribution to literature and photography, and in 2005 the Joseph Devaux Lifetime Achievement Award.

As a composer Charles Cadet (1924—) wasn't considered a member of the Arts Guild but his work was so directly connected with Roderick Walcott's playwriting that in spirit he was an integral part of the Guild. He composed all the scores of Roderick's musicals, including *Chanson Marianne, The Legend of Tom Fool, the Guitar Man's Song, The Wonderful World of Brother Rabbit,* and *Romiel Ec Juliette.* He also composed the music for *Tinday*, a play by McDonald Dixon. Besides theatrical scores, Charles Cadet has composed such popular songs as *Mass for Independence, Kyrie, A Dream of Freedom, Ode To An Artiste,* and *Poinsettia Blossom.* He was the first Recipient of the M&C Fine Arts Lifetime Achievement Award, and in 2005 was awarded The Saint Lucia Cross, the country's highest award, for distinguished and outstanding service. In 2015 he was inaugurated into the St. Lucia Cultural Icon Series.

By the time the Arts Guild folded, Novelist Garth St. Omer (1931 – 2018) had publish his three novels—*A*

Room on the Hill (1968), *Nor Any Country* (1969), and *J—*
, Black Bam and the Masqueraders (1972) —and his
three novellas or short stories—*The Lights on the Hill*
(1968) *Another Place Another Time* (1968) and *Syrop*
(1964) —that would claim him a place at the front line of
West Indian writers and would establish him as St.
Lucia's only internationally acclaimed novelist. As such
he was included in *Fifty Caribbean Writers: A Bio-
Bibliographical Critical Sourcebook* (1986), a collection of
essays on fifty major West Indian writers of the last two
centuries. Garth St. Omer has since published *Prismns*, a
novel published in 2016, and many short stories. He
served as Professor Emeritus of the English Department
at the University of California in Santa Barbara. In 2001
he was awarded St. Lucia Gold Medal of Merit for meri-
torious service in the fields of arts and literature.
Likewise, in 2005 he was awarded St. Lucia National Arts
Lifetime Achievement Award, and in 2017 he was
inducted into the St. Lucia Cultural Icon Series.

As playwright, screenwriter, painter, theatre director, costume and set designer, song lyricist and literary
editor, Roderick Walcott (1930-2000) was the driving
force behind the St. Lucia Arts Guild. He wrote seventeen plays and two screenplays and wrote the lyrics for
and helped compose eight musicals, in the process earn-
ing him the recognition as one of the founders of modern Caribbean theatre. "His play *The Harrowing of Benjy*

still remains the most produced play in the English-speaking Caribbean." Besides theatre, he led the Turks Steelband and is considered one of the pioneers of St. Lucian carnival. For his contributions to St. Lucian and Caribbean art and culture he was honored with Joseph Devaux Lifetime Achievement Award (2000), Order of the British Empire (OBE, 1976), and Saint Lucia Gold Medal of Honor (2000).

Dunstan St. Omer (1927 – 2015), a founding member of the Arts Guild, who as he said, served as an actor and set designer of the plays staged by the Guild, is one of St. Lucia's most renowned painters. He designed the St. Lucian flag and invented a new form of painting called Prismism. Beginning in the 1970s he revolutionized painting and the Roman Catholic Church in St. Lucia by creating altar piece murals populated by ordinary St. Lucian folk and images of the island's folk culture. His murals and beautification of the Cathedral of the Immaculate Conception in Castries has drawn international attention both to him and his country. Besides St. Lucia, he has painted murals in Mexico, Martinique and Trinidad. For his contributions to art and culture, Dunstan St. Omer was awarded Papal Medal of Merit (1985), St. Lucia Cross (2004), and Honorary Doctor of Letters (2009) from the University of the West Indies. In 2007 the Folk Research Center declared him a National Cultural Hero, then making him only the third cultural

Charles Cadet

icon to have received such an honor. And in 2010 he was invested with the Insignia of a Knight Commander of the Order of St. Michael and St. George (KCMG).

By 1971 Derek Walcott (1930 – 2017) had written no less than ten plays and had established the Trinidad Theatre Workshop that evolved into a world class theatre company. He had already published seven volumes of poetry including *25 Poems* (1948), *Epitaph for the Young : XII Cantos* (1949), *Poems* (1951), *In a Green Night: Poems 1948-1960* (1962), Selected Poems (1964), *The Castaway and Other Poems* (1965), and *The Gulf and Other Poems* (1969)—firmly establishing him as an inter-

Stanley French

nationally acclaimed poet. And by 2017, the year of his death, he had published over twenty-two volumes of poetry aggregated into 14 collections, written over 24 dramatic works many of which published in his eight collections of plays, and won at least twelve awards and prizes including Cholmondeley Award (1969), Obie Award for Best Foreign Play (for *Dream on Monkey*

Mountain, 1971), Officer of the Order of the British Empire (1972), MacArthur Foundation Fellowship Genius Award (1981), Queen's Gold Medal for Poetry (1988), Arts Council of Wales International Writers Prize (1990), WH Smith Literary Award (1990), Nobel Prize in Literature (1992), Honorary doctorate from the University of Essex (2008), T.S. Eliot Prize for Poetry (2011), OCM Bocas Prize for Caribbean Literature (2011), Griffin Trust For Excellence in Poetry Lifetime Recognition Award (2015), and Knight Commander of the Order of St. Lucia (2016).

However the outstanding achievements of the above mentioned members of the Arts Guild, they don't tell the complete story. Naturally most of the attention on the Arts Guild has been directed to the ones who created bodies of work in the form of plays, music, poetry and paintings by which their accomplishments can be evaluated by later generations. But by some accounts, the dancers, actors and actresses of the Arts Guild were just as distinguished and talented as the writers and painters, but we have no recordings of their performances, and lacking a film industry they didn't have the opportunity of gravitating into film as is sometimes the case in countries with an advance film industry.

Some of these other distinguished personalities of the St. Lucia Arts Guild include actresses Zin Theobalds, Teresa Plummer, Joan Lansiquot, Sixtus Jeanne Charles,

Pamela Walcott and Doris Thomas; actors Irvine John, Kenneth Monplaisir, Eric Branford, Arthur Jacobs, Oliver Oshaunessy, Carlton Glasgow, Hunter Francois, Frank Henry, Lennie St. Hill, Euralis Bouty and Irvin Norville; musicians and singers Frank Norville, Pet Gibson, Floreta Marquis, Ruby Yorke and Joyce Auguste; and set and costume designers Frantz Fritz, Michael Daniel and Shirley Edwards.

The accomplishments of the St. Lucia Arts Guild could not be considered a renaissance or a revolution if their spoils had been limited just to the Guild. But this was far from the case. Their many productions over a twenty-year period would have definitely developed or cultivated a heightened sense of art and culture among the Castries population. As an art educator for thirty years with the ministry of education charged with intro-ducing art in the island's school system, Dunstan St. Omer would have spread the artistic spirit and sensibili-ties of the Arts Guild throughout the country. His Roman Catholic Church murals that helped indigenize Catholicism in St. Lucia would have done no less a job of spreading the manifestations of the Arts Guild. And as a music supervisor for the St. Lucian school system and the leader of Hewanorra Voices, a major popular folk band in the 1970s, Joyce Auguste introduced folk music into the school curriculum.

The Arts Guild inspired and in some cases helped

develop the next generation of St. Lucian poets, novelist, playwrights, directors, photographers, painters and musicians, thus ensuring the continuity of what the Guild had started. Some of the more prominent of these second generation artists who the Arts Guild inspired included poets Jane King Hippolyte and Modeste Downes; novelists Michael Aubertin and Earl Long; dramatists George 'Fish' Alphonse, and Kennedy "Boots" Samuel; musicians Ronald "Boo" Hinckson and Luther Francois; painters Cedric George, Lugi St. Omer, Julio St. Omer, Giovanni St. Omer and Alwyn St Omer; poets and playwrights Kendal Hippolyte, Travis Weekes, Gandolph St. Clair, Melania Daniel, and Hazel Simmons-McDonald; poet, journalist and librarian John Robert Lee; and poet, playwright and event producer Adrian Augier.

These second generation of St. Lucian artists advanced the cause both as practitioners of their craft and by actively teaching and interacting with a younger generation of artists in the making. As English, literature, and drama lecturers at Sir Arthur Lewis Community College, which harbored students and teachers in train-ing from around the island, Allan Weekes , Jane King and Kendal Hippolyte had the opportunity to pass on their passion for the arts to several generations of the island's brightest. Added to that, over the years Kendal Hippolyte , McDonald Dixon, and John Robert Lee con-ducted poetry and theatre workshops , and their work

with the Writer's Forum, a Castries based open membership creative writers workshop, certainly helped create
the third and fourth generation of St. Lucia artist.

The hectic activity of the second generation of artists
is evident in the number of theatre undertakings that
succeeded the Arts Guild. These include The Creative
and Performing Arts Society, The New Day Theatre
Workshop, One Love Theatre, Unity Theatre Workshop,
Creole Theatre, Lighthouse Theatre, the Soufriere
Action Theatre and the State Theatre of Micoud. So in
both spirit and practice one can say the Arts Guild never
ended. It just took on different shapes.

Sometimes the legacy of the Arts Guild have flowed
from parents to off springs. Travis Weekes, the son of
Arts Guild playwright and director, Allan Weekes, has
become not only one of St. Lucia's most prolific playwrights and directors, but leads the way in St. Lucia
Creole Theatre. Dunstan St. Omer's four sons—Lugi,
Julio , Giovanni, and Alwyn— are now prominent St.
Lucian painters. Barbara Jacobs, daughter of Arthur
Jacobs, the famed Arts Guild actor, is the founder and
owner of Right Angle Imaging, an award winning marketing communications firm with several publications
including two magazines—*Island WHERE* and St. Lucia
Business *WHO's WHO*. Luther Francois, the son of musician, poet and educator, Hunter Francois, is widely considered the best musician St. Lucia has produced.

Mc Donald Dixon

The St. Lucia Arts Guild inspired not only the next generation of artists, but motivated the establishment of some of the key organizations that are helping to institutionalize the spirit of the Arts Guild and the essence of what Harold Simmons and the Guild was striving for. The two key institutions charged with preserving and advancing St. Lucian culture are the Folk Research Center and The Department of Culture renamed the Cultural Development Foundation.

Established in 1973 the Folk Research Center serves "as a repository for cultural heritage, a vehicle for research, study, recording and promulgating Saint Lucia's rich heritage." The Folk Research Centre was founded by Msgr. Dr. Patrick Anthony, a second generation Arts Guild cultural activities, and since inception has had at its head various second generation Arts Guild artists.

Similarly the Department of Culture or the Cultural Development Foundation was established by government "to promote the development and management of the arts and culture in St. Lucia." Roderick Walcott served as the first executive director of the department, and since then second generation Arts Guild exponents have invariably held that position.

The legacy and spirit of Harold Simmons and the St. Lucia Arts Guild continues to not only inspire St. Lucian artists and cultural activities but also to permeate the country's educational and cultural institutions and all levels of St. Lucian society. Therefore, without a doubt, the St. Lucia Arts Guild unleashed nothing less than a cultural renaissance.

But unaware of all this history, the 1993 banana farmers, themselves making history, went on a strike that brought deaths in the valley and the transformation of the banana industry in St. Lucia.

18

A Revolution

Tourism may have replaced bananas as king, but it wasn't the only sector that had undermined the reign of bananas. So too did manufacturing, the third pillar (the other two being agriculture and tourism) upon which, according to the vision of Mr. John Compton, the country's economy would stand. Consistent with that vision, not only did the government extend tax exemptions and other generous concessions to attract foreign manufacturing enterprises but in a leap of faith it took the initiative and built a host of factory shells to house the manufacturers that were coming. The government took even further steps to ensure the success of its vision. It designated Vieux Fort the industrial capital of the country, the centerpiece of its manufacturing vision. Few could have questioned the government's choice of an industrial capital. Blessed with air and seaport, a well-developed road system, and an expanse of flat land the likes of which seen no where else on the island, for an industrial complex Vieux Fort was a natural.

With factory shells in place, a designated industrial capital, and generous incentive packages, led by Winera and the Windward and Leeward Brewery, the manufacturing vision of Mr. John Compton soon became a reality. Between 1977 and 1990, the contribution of manufacturing to real GDP grew by an annual average of more than 9 percent, from EC$26 million or 6 percent of GDP to EC$78 million, representing 8 percent of GDP.

In the 1990s the industry experienced some difficulties. The output of the paper and paperboard manufacturing subsector fell by more than half due to a failing banana industry, the country's main user of cardboard boxes. Similarly, the island's garment production fell by nearly a third as many of the foreign-owned garment assembly firms fled to lower labor cost CARICOM, Latin American and Asian countries and to Mexico after the signing of the North American Free Trade Agreement.

So, compared with the near double-digit annual percent growth rate of the previous decade, because of the misfortunes of those two sub sectors, the contribution of the manufacturing sector to real GDP declined by an annual average of more than 1 percent.

Nonetheless, in 1993, the year that banana farmers went on the strike that shocked the nation, with a manufacturing sector contributing EC$82 million to real GDP, compared to banana's EC$72 million, like tourism, manufacturing eclipsed bananas. Right up to 1999 manufacturing still held steady. The 173 manufacturing enterprises in operation employed 4,325 workers, or more than 7 percent of all employed workers, contributed 6 percent or EC$85 million to GDP and generated $47 million of exports, or 29 percent of all exports.

Those factories spewed out galvanized sheets, plastic shopping bags, detergents, industrial glue, body filler, cardboard boxes, furniture, garments, men's briefs, women's under garments, soft drinks, ketchup, food seasoning, juice concentrates, electronic delay lines, thermistors, transistors, resisters, transformers, bottled water, packaged food for airline service, beers, malts, gifts and other novelties. To Barbados, the OECS, America, Europe, these products find their way.

In keeping with Mr. Compton's vision of turning Vieux Fort into the industrial capital of St. Lucia, a disproportionate number of the factories are to be found in

Vieux Fort. This industrialization of Vieux Fort has been of tremendous benefit, not just to the town, but to the whole south. In fact, industrial along with population growth has greatly spurred the town's commercial sector. By the late nineties, several new banks had opened their doors, several long established banks had moved into larger and improved buildings and many Castries-based businesses had opened branches in Vieux Fort.

One suspects that when the UWP government first dreamed up the island's tripartite economic plan (agriculture, tourism and manufacturing) it only had in mind an economic transformation. Nevertheless, what the factories did was to bring together young ladies, secondary school graduates or not, from all corners of the island. There, on the factory floor, they meet, bringing news from their corners of the island, sharing their common problems, discussing the nature of men. For the first time young ladies, instead of sitting at home waiting for nothingness, are marching into the workforce, empowering themselves economically and socially. No longer do they need a lover to afford shoes on their feet. Empowered, they can force men to wear condoms, and tell those who measure their manhood by how many women they sleep with to get lost. So what is happening is not just an economic transformation, but also a social and political revolution. Not on the scale Karl Max had envisioned, but a revolution nonetheless whose full implications are yet to be determined.

The women do not make much money. Up to the year 2002, three, four or five hundred dollars per month was the norm, and after deducting money for clothes and shoes (because unlike staying at home one has to look good when one goes to work), and then $100 for lunch and transportation, and also government deductions, they were left with less than $300. No wonder many young men, full of machismo, prefer to remain idle than subject themselves to what they consider slave wages. Nevertheless, the women, unhindered by testosterone and generally more practical than men, reckoned that $200 or $300 was better than zero, especially when staying at home meant endless washing, cooking and cleaning for the same young men who instead of finding jobs were glorying in idleness and marijuana.

Hurray for the women, but sad for the nation, because what is happening on the factory floors isn't an isolated incident but just one aspect, maybe the smaller aspect, of what is happening regarding the progressiveness of women relative to men in the country. If one were to take a walk down the streets of Vieux Fort or Castries on business days, one would see multitudes of smartly dressed young women on high heels, heads in the air, and eyes that seem to say that unlike the song, *no where to go, nothing to do, I have places to go and plenty of things to do.* The young men one would see in that kind of business mode are few and far. It seems that before long only women will be running St. Lucia, and the women will be so far ahead of the men that they will have to start importing their spouses. Maybe an over-seas ad will read like this: *Looking for a man (no matter the age) who is willing to hold a job (it doesn't matter what kind of job and how much the job earns), who isn't on crack and doesn't smoke too much marijuana, and who doesn't feel to be a man is to carry a gun.*

As with tourism and bananas, manufacturing has come with some baggage. Besides the goods the facto-ries produce for the home market and beyond, they pro-duce "bads" for the land and its people. The "bads" are called pollution. Where the agricultural pesticides, weedicides, fungicides, and nematicides left off, factory waste has taken over. Year after year, with almost no voices of protest, factory sludge is making its way down into the nation's rivers and ocean. In certain parts of Vieux Fort's industrial zone permanent factory stenches hang in the air, and the colors of some nearby streams changes depending on which factory is pumping waste at the time. In some factories the nation's young women, most in the prime of their childbearing years, are daily exposed to harmful chemicals. One wonders whether ten, twenty years from now, the nation will have to contend with an epidemic of deformed births?

Another of the evils of manufacturing is that factories are threatening to take over the nation's agricultural lands. For example, going full speed ahead, and as if intent on hammering the final nail in the coffin of bananas, factories are now sitting on the fertile lands of Union, in the North of Castries, on which many an agricultural student learned how to grow crops. And at Odsan, just South of the Cul-de-Sac Valley, factories are sitting in the middle of banana fields. The hotels have taken over the beaches. It seems the factories are intent on taking over the farms.

Factories, however, are not the only cause of the disappearance of the country's farm lands. Land hungry, Castries is gradually moving into the Cul-de-Sac Valley. The newly opened, four mile, seventy-five million dollar Tunnel Highway turned Millennium Highway that takes one to the valley by avoiding the messy and slow business of climbing and descending the Morne yet gives one a lovely view of the Hess part of the Caribbean Sea, and makes one feel that suddenly one has entered a big country, will do nothing but hasten the buildup of the valley. Moreover, given the rate of household formation along the Vieux Fort-Castries Highway, between the Barré de l'Isle and Dennery, it may not be long before the La Caye and Mabouya valleys are swallowed up. Soon there might be nothing left for the farmers of the Mabouya Valley to strike over. The once fertile Balembouche estate, situated between Piaye and

Choiseul, Vieux Fort aside, probably the largest stretch of flat land in the south, is being chopped up into residential parcels. Soon, most of the island's agricultural valleys near population centers will be gobbled up. The odds, it seems, are against bananas in particular and agriculture in general. Clearly, a national land use plan is long over due.

19

A Nation in Trouble

Despite the growth of the tourism and manufacturing sectors, if bananas are in trouble then the nation maybe in even greater trouble. In 1999, with a real per capita GDP of over EC$7500, the World Bank pronounced St. Lucia an upper-middle income country, allowing it to join the ranks of Barbados, Trinidad and Israel, and showing that the nation had reached a new plateau in its development march. However, therein lies the country's dilemma. In its initial stages of development, given where it was starting from, a flourishing banana industry, a rising tourism sector and low wage manufacturing enterprises combined with international aid, were sufficient to spearhead acceptable economic growth rates. But as a middle income country (and the accompanying higher wage structure that comes along with it), low wage, low skill, footloose factories, the production and export of bananas, a soil depleting and environmentally degrading raw product, and a fickle tourism sector whose economic benefit to the country is questionable at best (given the current trend of cruise ship tourism and inclusive hotels and the fact that a large portion of tourists expenditures do not remain in the host country), may not be sufficient for sustained economic growth, especially since none of these activities help develop high-level skills that in turn could spur high wage, high tech industries. Furthermore, as the country's standard of living rises, international donors will be less forthcoming with aid.

This suggests that the only way St. Lucia can continue to enjoy high rates of economic growth would be to keep improving its level of productivity. After all, it is a well-known fact that an industry's or a country's wage rate is directly linked with its level of productivity. A country's level of productivity can be improved by the adoption of new and improved technology (or alternatively, increasing and improving its stock of physical capital) and by improving the quality of its human resource or, in the jargon of development economists, investing in its human capital. Human capital can be improved by education, training, and the cultivation of attitudes and habits conducive to sound business practices.

Regarding education and training, the nation has a mountain to climb. The 1995 census indicated that over 27 percent of St. Lucians were illiterate. Yet if functional illiteracy was taken into account, the illiteracy statistic would climb even higher. History has taught us that education, the accumulation of knowledge, has always been critical for the progress of humanity. Besides contributing directly to technological advancements, education enables us to be more productive because it increases our capacity for learning, it makes us more adaptable to change, and it makes it easier for us to overcome inherent prejudices and idiosyncrasies that hamper our ability to function in the work place and society in general.

If in the past education was essential for our progress, then today it is even more so because we have entered a new age in history—the age of the information and computing revolution. The essential nature of the industrial revolution was that machine power had replaced many tasks done by man and beast, and as a result how society went about producing goods and services changed and the speed at which it did so increased tremendously.

As the name implies, the essential character of the

information revolution is information. Because of the computer society is generating, analyzing and storing greater volumes of information, and at unprecedented speeds. Consequently, the mode and speed of producing goods and services have changed, the way people interact has changed, the way people speak has changed, even the way people think has changed. The scare that surrounded the Y2K phenomenon was a clear indication of how pervasive the computer has become in people's daily lives. The computer flies aircrafts, controls vehicles, runs electronic devices and home appliances. Banks use it to record and store information on savings, loans and deposits. The government uses it to track births, deaths, and taxes. Teachers use it to prepare their lessons. Doctors use it to perform operations.

In the industrial revolution it was machines and industrial processes that drove the revolution. In the information revolution it is computers and information systems. One can think of the computer as hardware and software. Hardware concerns the wiring of the computer, it is everything one sees when one looks inside a computer. Software is what one doesn't see. Software is a set of instructions that directs the computer into doing certain tasks. Without software the computer can do nothing. If the computer is at the center of the information revolution, then software is at the center of what the computer does. Still, what is the essential character of software? Software is nothing more than encoded instructions, encoded information, encoded knowledge. So essentially knowledge is what is driving this revolution, and this is why education, the accumulation of knowledge, is more important to the economic well-being of nations than ever before.

It is true that knowledge was also what drove the industrial revolution, but it was knowledge as translated into machines and processes. In the information revolution it is knowledge as translated into knowledge. Knowledge is the beginning and the end, the objective and the goal, the motive and the action.

In days gone by nations counted their wealth by how much territory and natural resources they commanded and how many slaves and serfs they possessed. As the Soviet Union found out, although the hard way, that is no longer the case. The ongoing revolution has shifted the basis of wealth from that of natural resources to that of knowledge, information, and technology. If one has any doubt of that, look at Japan. The second world war started when Germany, headed by Hitler, started invading and taking over other European countries. Italy and Japan sided with Hitler, and the rest of the world combined forces against them. Japan's interest in the war was in taking over countries in the Pacific to gain access to raw materials. Japan, Italy and Germany were defeated, and Japan and Europe were devastated. In fact, the war against Japan ended after the Americans dropped atomic bombs on the Japanese cities of Hiroshima and Nagasaki. Japan realized that it had lost the war to America because of superior American technology. So after the war, aided ironically by America, Japan embarked on a massive industrialization and technological program. They took western machines and products apart and learned to make them better. They sent people to Europe and America to watch, ask questions, photograph and tape-record technological information. Japan's concerted efforts at gaining technological knowledge paid off handsomely. In 1950, five years after the war, Japan made only 32,000 vehicles, which amounted to less than two days of American manufacture. Yet by 1980, Japan was exporting six million vehicles, and had surpassed America as the biggest car maker in the world. Today Japan is a clear world leader in auto technology. Before 1945, "Made in Japan" meant low quality, inferiority, but by the 1980's "Made in Japan" was associated with quality, class, top performance. Japan produces not only cars but most high-tech goods. They make computers, cameras, precision machinery and instruments, robotics and electronics. So successful has Japan become, that by the 1990s it had become the second largest economy in the world, second only to the United States.

In this new era, never before have small nation

states like St. Lucia been so well positioned. Because if there be one thing the shift of the basis of wealth creation from natural resources to knowledge has done is to level off the playing field. Suddenly, anyone with a computer and a modem, be it in the middle of the banana field, has access to the same information as someone on Wall Street, in the middle of Manhattan, in the middle of New York City, the heartthrob of America.

No country epitomizes this new revolution than America, and no company than Microsoft. Pick up any one of Microsoft's software products and what you would hold in your hand is a compact disc (CD), a piece of metal thinner than a coin and no larger than a saucer, a piece of metal worth mere pennies. Yet by the year 2000 Microsoft was generating more than twenty billion dollars in annual revenues, placing it among the 100 largest companies in the US. Bill Gates, its founder and principal owner, was reported to be the richest private individual in the world. So what about those CD's that is so valuable? It is the information stored on them, information that drives computers, information that drives the computing world. Information, that's all it is. More than 80 percent of computers in the world use the Microsoft software that runs computers, the software that all other software interface with, the software that acts as the language or better yet the operating system of the computer. That operating system is called

Windows.

So how did this company called Microsoft and that software called Windows begin? It all began when Bill Gates and a few of his buddies got hold of an old computer and started tinkering with it in his parents' basement. So what Is the implication of all this to St. Lucia? It means that any one of the nation's students now gracing the classrooms of the secondary schools can start tinkering with a computer, and then twenty years later St. Lucia could have a computer software company generating billions of dollars and rivaling, surpassing even, the Microsofts of the world. For it doesn't take natural resources, it doesn't require a great deal of electricity, initially it doesn't require a large capital outlay. All the student needs is a computer and some knowledge.

Many large companies in the US out source some of their computer programming to programers in India and in some ex-states of the Soviet Union. Via e-mail, the companies explain what is needed, and again via E-mail computer programmers in these countries send back the completed programs. Both parties benefit. The US companies cut employee cost by not having to provide medical and other employee benefits, and the Indian programmers get US salaries without ever having to leave home. There is nothing to prevent St. Lucians from entering into such arrangements with US companies.

Nothing except having the necessary programing skills and the relevant knowledge.

If this era represents the best of times for small, resource-poor states like St. Lucia, then it may also represent the worse of times. Aided by computers, national, cultural and market boundaries are rapidly disappearing. Now every six months the makers of computers are coming out with faster and more versatile computers. Every day some company comes out with a new computer and electronic gadget. It is said that human knowledge doubles every five years. Yet only a generation ago estimates suggested that the total of human knowledge was doubling every fourteen years. Clearly, history has been placed on a runaway train. The peril St. Lucia faces is that knowledge and information are being generated at such unprecedented rates that how much information one needs and the education required to function well are much greater than before and are increasing. Yet a 27 percent illiteracy rate is staring the nation in the face. And in talking about international competitiveness, the issue is not just about being able to read and write, it is about how many college graduates and technologically savvy workers the country has at its disposal.

The trouble in which the country finds itself because of a largely uneducated population, however, goes beyond the ability to attract high tech enterprises. Lack of education is exacting a tremendous cost on the nation. Many are not only illiterate or functionally illiterate but can barely understand English, the country's official language. So much so that businesses, the government, and just about any institution that deals with the public have to spend vast amounts of resources on just trying to explain to citizens the simplest of procedures and policies. Institutions cannot simply print brochures and expect the public to be informed. When it comes to loans, bank accounts, etc., banks have to arbitrarily make decisions for some of their clients because the fine points of such things as the computation of interest are beyond the grasps of many. People are robbed without even knowing that they are being robbed. The extent to which people misinterpret government policies makes one wonder how can the country go forward with that level of ignorance.

The lack of education puts a tremendous burden on management. For things to go smoothly even the simplest of tasks has to be managed to the last detail. It would be interesting to find out how often things have to be redone, how much delay, how much waste that results from the inability of people to understand and follow directions. It may not be far fetched to suggest that education or the lack of it accounts for over half the country's problems. It is surprising that St. Lucia has reached that far with such a low level of education. But the country's good luck might be running out. Despite the malls that are mushrooming, the cars that are running out of roads, and the mansions springing on hilltops, it will soon be futile talking about further development without a focus on education. Moreover, education represents the country's only chance of surmounting its historical baggage.

One thing that strikes a visitor to St. Lucia is the youthfulness of its population. Nearly a third of the population is under the age of fifteen. On school days the sight of multitudes of children in pink and brown, black and white, yellow and grey, orange and checkered, some bobbing and weaving among traffic, some emerging from the banana foliage, some skipping along rural roads, full of motion, sound and eagerness, may remind one of when the world was freshly created. Yet one cannot but worry about what is going to happen to all these young people in this information age. How is the nation going to occupy all of them when already so many school leavers cannot find jobs? When, even in its best years of economic performance, the unemployment rate hovers above 15 percent? How is the nation educating them, preparing them to be competitive in this global economy?

Bananas may not be king anymore, but given the existing level of education, the nation is ill equipped to move beyond bananas, beyond the stitching of garments at footloose factories, and beyond smiling

"Simply Beautiful" to tourist. It appears, once again, that history will prevail.

It was probably because the 1993 banana farmers were unaware of all this that they had made a miscalculation, therefore giving credence to the saying that a people who are unaware of their history will self-destruct. Probably farmers hadn't realized that so much had changed since bananas first took root on the island. Clearly they had overestimated their value to the nation. They were sure that they were too precious, too indispensable to the nation to be shot, killed, done away with. If they had studied history, it would have shown them the error of their self importance. They would have realized that the world had changed, the people had changed, the economy had changed, the Prime Minister, though still a banana farmer, the same one who forty years earlier had risked a thrusting police bayonet, and the pointed gun of the owner of the Dennery sugar factory, all in the interest of farmers, had changed. The nation had so much else on its mind that the plight of farmers had become the least of its concerns. Seemingly unaware of history and believing in an illusion farmers went on a strike and things fell apart.

20

The Funerals

The funerals were sad and beautiful. Beautiful but sad. Two farmers sacrificed to the banana god. Martyred. The nation watched with teary eyes. Some probably wondered: "Did it have to happen? Couldn't it have been stopped? Wasn't there a better way? Why did the farmers have to be so stubborn?" "*Pò djab!*" they probably said. "*Pò djab!*"

In grief, at no other time were the farmers so noble, so godlike. Like Christ on the crucifixion cross they had paid the ultimate price, the ultimate sacrifice. For of what greater honor there is than a man giving up his life for a cause?

The funerals were national affairs. Motorcades of farmers originating as far as Micoud, with great pageantry and fanfare, joined their comrades in the valley, helping to mourn and bury their fallen brethren. The people, many waving placards calling for justice and the resignation of the Prime Minister, himself a banana farmer, came out in masses, causing traffic jams and chaos in the valley. Many were dressed in the same clothes that they wore when working under the bananas. Clothes blanketed with dark brown stains with which the banana had proclaimed the farmers his forever, because no matter how hard the farmers tried and with what—Tide, Breeze, Clorox—nothing could get the banana out. Others carried various parts of the banana plant (from the leaves to the whole tree) to the funeral, as if to say our brothers may be dead, banana prices may be down, the SLBGA may be unbelievably corrupt, the Prime Minister, himself a banana farmer, may not care, the country may not care, the whole damn world may not care, but as sure as there is a God bananas shall never die. Some other mourners were dressed in outfits made out of banana trash, as if dressed for a masquerade, proving that they were not just farmers and engineers but they were fashion designers too.

The churches were too small to hold the funerals. In the Catholic Church where the first funeral was held, mourners swamped the main isle and the altar behind which a crucified Christ looked on. But His words: *Father, forgive them; for they know not what they do,* when it was His turn to pay the ultimate sacrifice, fell on deaf ears, because intermittently cries of pain and anger denouncing the Prime Minister, himself a banana farmer, pierced through the church, disturbing the funeral service.

Some young farmers, as if to say that the funeral service was too morbid for their taste, and that they too wished for martyrdom, by passed the church altogether, and using the front of the police station as their stage, and a handful of silent, somber policemen dressed in fatigues as their audience, enacted the scene in which the farmers met their deaths, proving not only were farmers engineers and fashion designers but they were actors too. Not to be out done, in church, another young man presented arms with a banana bunch.

The second farmer was buried on Sunday next to his comrade in death who was buried the day before. He was placed in his grave in the same hour that darkness started to engulf the nation. And as if bidding him farewell, the sky opened and let down a light shower of rain. Lying in their graves, the farmers were not alone. They had just joined the chain of the thousands of their ancestors who had died on the march to the African coast, the millions that died on the transatlantic journey to the sugar plantations, the thousands who had died premature deaths toiling sweats of pain on the plantations, the hundreds killed or maimed trying to escape into the hills, the eight sugar workers shot dead in 1849 when the government invoked the Mutiny Act for workers revolting against unlivable wages and deplorable working conditions, the four dead and twenty-three wounded workers that resulted when a company of 22 policemen fired into a crowd of striking workers in the Cul-de-Sac valley in 1907.

Alive, farmers may have been unmindful of history, but now dead history had claimed them as its very own.

References

Bryan, Jami. "Fighting for Respect: African-American Soldiers in WWI." MilitaryHistoryOnline.com.Web. 27 June 2013.

Charles, George F.L. 1994. The History of the Labor Movement in St. Lucia, 1945-1974: A personal Memoir. Castries: Folk Research Center.

D. Sinclair DaBreo. 1981. Of Men and Politics: The Agony of St. Lucia. Castries, St. Lucia: Commonwealth Publishers International Ltd.

Economic and Social Review. Various issues. Government of St. Lucia.

Gachet, Charles. 1975. a history of the Roman Catholic Church in St. Lucia. Port of Spain, Trinidad: Key Caribbean Publications.

Hall, Douglas. 1982. The Caribbean Experience: An Historical Survey 1450-1960. Heinemann CXC History. London: Heinemann.

Harmsen, Jolien. 1999. Sugar, Slavery and Settlement: A social history of Vieux Fort St. Lucia, from the Amer-indians to the present. Castries: Folk Research Center.

Jesse, Charles. 1994 (1956). Outline of St. Lucia's History. Castries: St. Lucia Historical and Archeological Society.

Khan, Nasser. "Legendary labour Leaders." Guardian Media Ltd. Trinidad & Tobago Guardian Online, 20 June 2011. Web. 27 June 2013
King, Bruce. 1995. West Indian Literature. 2nd ed. London: Macmillan Educational Ltd.

Memorial Gates Trust. "Caribbean participants in the First World War." Memorial Gates Trust. Web. 27 June 2013.

References

Mintz, Sidney W. and Richard Price. 1992. The Birth of African-American Culture: An anthropological perspective. Boston: Beacon Press.

Nurse, Keith and W. Sandford. 1995. Windward Islands Bananas: Challenges and Options Under the Single European Market. Kingston Jamaica: Friedrich Ebert Stiftung,

Paquet, Pouchet S. 1995. "The Fifties." West Indian Literature. Ed. Bruce King. London: Macmillan Educational Ltd,. 51-62.

Reynolds, Anderson. 2001. Death by Fire. (A Novel) New York: Jako Books.

Reynolds, Anderson.. 2000. "A School Waiting to be Rescued." The Mirror, October 13, 20 and 27, and November 3 and 10.

Reynolds, Anderson. 2000. "The Taming of Vieux Fort." The Mirror, June 9, 16, 23 and 30.

Reynolds, Anderson.1992. "As Goes Bananas, So Does St. Lucia's Economy" The Voice, March 19, 21, and 24.

Reynolds, Philip K. 1927. The Banana: Its History, Cultivation and Place among Staple Foods. Boston and New York: Houghton Mifflin Company.

Serieux, John E. 1986. "Human Settlement In A Modified Plantation Economy: The Case of St. Lucia." Master's Thesis. Cornell, New York: Cornell University.

Simkin, John. "Britain in 1914." Spartacus Educational. Sept. 1997. Web. 23 June 2013.

The Voice. 1993. Various articles on the 1993 banana strike in the October issues. Castries, St. Lucia.

Ramchand, Kenneth. 1970. The West Indian Novel and its Background. London: Farber & Farber.
Vitalis, David. 1993. "The P.M. Bungled Badly." Castries, St. Lucia: The Voice, October 16.

Vitalis, David. 1993. "Bloody Thursday: Could All This Have Been Avoided." Castries, St. Lucia: The Voice, October 9.

Vitalis, David. 1993. "Banana War Goes Local." Castries, St. Lucia: The Voice, October 2.

The World of Anderson Reynolds

"Death by Fire is an impressive piece of narration ... A veritable tapestry of St. Lucian life and culture ... Easily one of the most compelling pieces of literature I have laid hands on in recent years."
—**Modeste Downes, author of *Phases***

"The telling of the story is exceptional ... A cunningly-woven tale ... A journey back into St. Lucian life ... (which) paints the dark side of the struggle for survival in a young country."
— **The Voice**

"A novel on a grand scale ... A broad canvas of St. Lucian life ... If one is looking for a key to the feeling and conscience of the age in which we live, this novel is a guide."
—**The Crusader**

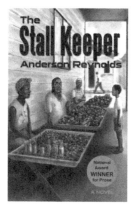

The Stall Keeper is an engaging narrative that readers of all ages will find both informative and climactic... An excellent aid to our understanding of our past."
— **The Voice**

In Dr. Reynolds St. Lucia has produced another writer of the calibre, or of even deeper essence than Nobel Laureate V. S. Naipaul ...
— **Peter Lansiquot, CARICOM economist and diplomat**

"The Stall Keeper is arguably the best novel to come out of St. Lucia."
— **Mc Donald Dixon, novelist, poet, and playwright**

"... a wonderful journey down memory lane for anyone who has breathed the salty sea breeze of Vieux Fort in the middle and late 20th century... It's a wry book; a story that sticks in the mind."
— **Jolien Harmsen, author of A History of St. Lucia**

My Father Is No Longer There

Anderson Reynolds

"Dr. Reynold's mastery as a fierce storyteller is yet again reaffirmed. This memoir calmly and thoroughly takes the reader along the rough terrain of a family's epic struggle for survival..."
— **Peter Lansiquot, CARICOM diplomat and Economist**

"A pulsating ... riveting ... and compellingly readable narrative."
— **Modeste Downes, author of A Lesson on Wings.**

"A love ballad, a joy to read and a privilege to be savoured."
— **Dr. Jolien Harmsen, author of A History of St. Lucia.**

www.jakoproductions.com

Other Jako Books

The Brown Curtains embroils readers in a steaming love story involving Raj, an Indo Guyanese emigrant to St. Lucia, and Felicity, an Afro-St. Lucian beauty. The only question is whether their love can withstand the racial and religous bigotry of Raj's parents.

"Whether you are Black, Indian, Christian, Hindu or Moslem, The Brown Curtains gently goads you in the direction of forgotten trails and alleys of the diaspora. It is a novel for everyone because it shows that adapting to a new life is the same wherever you arrive."
—Michael Aubertin, Author, *Neg Maron: Freedom Fighters*

The Brown Curtains is a novel of great humor, and philosophical and intellectual insight."
— Allan Weekes, Author of *Talk of the Devil*

"Phases is a collection of over fifty dew-drenched poems that speaks powerfully to a past when living was peaceful and growing up was fun, and a present whose dynamic invokes nostalgia and a craving for a return to the past."
—Augustus Cadette, author of *In My Craft*

"Some of Modeste Downes' poems are acrid, like the taste of the sea-grapes that festoon the beaches of Vieux Fort. Others are nostalgic, insightful, cynical, bold, but all elements of a veritable feast."
—Michael Aubertin, author of *Neg Maron: Freedom Fighters*

"Like the works of Derek Walcott, Phases lifts us from the deepest woe to the highest contemplation of what life could be ...Downes is a nationalistic and romantic poet with echoes of William Wordsworth, and Oliver Goldsmith and Phases is reminiscent of Derek Walcott's *Another Life.*"
— Jacques Compton, Author of *a troubled dream*

(A Lesson On Wings) is a compilation of extraordinary poetic work ... an enthralling mixture of poetic genres ... destined to be heralded as one of the all-time great collections of Caribbean poetry ... no home or school library should be without a volume of this work.
— **Victor Marquis, author of *Search* and *The Adventures of Lennie Zandoli***

Modeste Downes is a master of the craft that builds narrative tapestries ... He embraces the entire palette of emotions and finds words to embody them all ... His use of language is impressive ... (and his) easy blend of Kweyol, Latin, 'high' English and profanity works like a dream ... You cannot get more St. Lucia-in-your-face than this. It is a brilliant collection of poems. Buy it. Read it. Share it.
—**Jolien Harmsen, author of *A History of St. Lucia,* and *Rum Justice***

www.jakoproductions.com

Anderson Reynolds was born and raised in Vieux Fort, St. Lucia, where he now resides. He holds a PhD in Food and Resource Economics from the University of Florida. He is the author of two other award-winning and national best-selling books, namely the novel *Death by Fire* and the creative nonfiction *The Struggle For Survival: an historical, political, and socioeconomic perspective of St. Lucia*. Dr. Reynolds' books and newspaper and magazine articles have established him as one of St. Lucia's most prominent and prolific writers and a foremost authority on its socioeconomic history.